Corporate Deception

Corporate Deception
A True Story

GILBERT A. PEREIRA

CORPORATE DECEPTION
Copyright @ 2012 Gilbert A Pereira
ISBN: 979-865-75-8689-3

Publisher
Gilbert A Pereira
Email: gil_pere@yahoo.com.sg
Website: https://www.GilbertPereira.com
Tel: +65 9383 2472

Disclaimer
Any resemblance of "lawyer personalities" in the quotes/cartoons
to lawyers who are living, dying or dead is **not coincidental**.
Those who can relate themselves to any of them are advised to
consume it in the right spirit and/or with the right spirit. Not
every lawyer deserves the disdain of these quotes/cartoons.
Undeniably, there are those who deserve our respect for the ethical
values they advocate whilst discharging their duties for their clients
and at the same time upholding their principled obligations as
officers of the Court.

Dedicated to my late wife
Sujatha Renata Pereira
13 Oct 1961 – 1 Jan 2013

Personally, I don't think you can make a lawyer honest by an act of legislature. You've got to work on his conscience. And his lack of a conscience is what makes him a lawyer.

Will Rogers

CONTENTS

"By the way, our legal firm was wondering if you paid up on your invoice"

FOREWORD

There was a time when I thought that law and justice were one and the same thing. Not anymore. That is not to say that law can exist independent of justice. It cannot; because a legal system bereft of justice, will lack legitimacy and ultimately be disregarded by society at large. For legal systems and the laws they administer to have value and legitimacy, they must contain some normative content, whether that content be informed by religion or some other ethical or moral foundation. Thus, criminal law will not be obeyed if it is blatantly unfair or makes no sense. We should not be allowed to criminalize behaviour that has no effect or bearing on society at large. So a person can be charged for wearing no clothes but cannot be deemed a criminal if all he wore was black in colour. The former impacts society's sensibilities and sense of decency and morality while the latter does not.

Yet, even within systems as well-regarded and well-administered as Singapore, things can go horribly wrong – as it did for *Gilbert Pereira*. That is because laws are general in application and are necessarily drafted in wide terms. Such generality is good because it allows the law to cover all the bases, so to speak. However, it also allows those who would manipulate the laws to their own ends an avenue for exploitation.

Lawyers have a sacred duty to act in the best interests of their clients – in accordance with the law. But the law cannot guard against negligent or crooked lawyers; at least not pre-emptively, for there exists no system for us to peer into the hearts of men. The law can provide for avenues of remedy after the dastardly deed is done. By then, it is often too late. The damage is done, and faith in the law and the legal system is lost.

The best legal system must have the best laws; and by that, I mean laws that are responsive to society's ever-changing needs. But above all, it needs the best people to run the system, and by this, I do not mean the cleverest people, but those with the highest integrity and sense of justice. Only then will the twain – law and justice – meet.

Kenneth Chan*
*not his real name – as he doesn't want unwarranted attention – is a renowned law professor from the National University of Singapore)

PREFACE

When *Signode (S) Pte Ltd*, a business entity of Fortune 500 Company *Illinois Tool Works Inc.*, engaged the services of my company, *Absolute Tec & Services Pte Ltd*, we thought we had found an aristocratic client that we could showcase in our clientele list. Little did we expect its transformation to an ungrateful client after the successful close of our assignment. An arduous legal battle ensued where *Signode* disputed an outstanding amount of S$152,000.00 due to us as professional fees. This book reveals the extent *Signode* went to avoid paying our rightful dues and uncovers how its lawyers, **Messrs David Lim & Partners muddled the issues when its consultant, *Kroll*, had ascertained that we were entitled to the disputed fees**.

Instead of respecting *Kroll's* findings and advising *Signode* accordingly (which would have cut legal costs drastically), Messrs *David Lim & Partners* submitted false evidence in Court, stating that an agreement to appoint *Kroll* to ascertain whether *Absolute* was entitled to the disputed fees was a concoction. However, *Signode* admitted appointing *Kroll* and said it was not to ascertain whether the disputed fees was genuine but to investigate *Absolute's* claim as part of a due diligence exercise, in contemplation of legal proceedings. This was utter rubbish, dignified with legal jargon to mislead the Court.

Having stated that, *Signode* **feared to submit the findings of** ***Kroll*** **to the Court (which would have exposed its lies and the false submission of its high-heeled lawyers),** claiming that the said findings were privileged information – another legal mumbo jumbo. *Absolute's* lawyers, *Messrs Vijay & Company* urged the Court to order a trial so that witnesses could be called and evidence examined to determine whether the agreement to appoint *Kroll* was indeed a concoction. However, *Messrs David Lim & Partners* argued successfully for a summary judgment, stating that even if the agreement to appoint *Kroll* was genuine, *Absolute* was not entitled to its outstanding fees based on legal technicalities.

Factually, *Signode* owed *Absolute,* but legally *Absolute* cannot claim this debt. This conundrum led to my earlier publication titled, FACTUALLY YES, LEGALLY NO! – a joke book on lawyers and their antics in Court.

CORPORATE DECEPTION is not a novel. It is a case book that dwells deeper into this *David versus Goliath* struggle, with undisputable facts and shocking insights into the double-dealing, corporate sleight-of-hand and legal manipulation that a big corporation used to pervert the client-provider relationship with a smaller company.

Gilbert A Pereira

"I didn't really want to become a
lawyer, but career opportunities
are limited for a person who is
completely lacking scruples."

CHAPTER 1

THE ASSIGNMENT

Sometime in February 1998, *CS Packaging Corporation (S) Pte Ltd* (a joint venture company between *Cyklop (S) Pte Ltd* and *Gerrard-Signode Pte Ltd)*, now known as *Signode (S) Pte Ltd*, engaged the services of *Absolute Tec & Services Pte Ltd*, a private investigation agency duly licensed by the Singapore Police Force, to carry out investigations on its Managing Director who was suspected of breaching his fiduciary duties. *Signode's* suspicion on its Managing Director arose after its headquarters in Chicago received an anonymous letter, citing grave business irregularities (Appendix 1).

    Signode informed *Absolute* that its Managing Director had submitted his notice of resignation and was continuing to serve the company as his last day of work was six months from the date of notice. The objective of the assignment for *Absolute* was to gather sufficient evidence to establish *Signode's* Managing Director had breached his fiduciary duties – which would then enable *Signode* to legally forfeit a handsome gratuity payment due to him on his last day of work. *Signode* was of the opinion that this gratuity amount was going to be used as working capital by its Managing Director in a rival company that he had set up to compete against *Signode* upon his resignation.

A man who never graduated from school might steal from a freight car. But a man who attends college and graduates as a lawyer might steal the whole railroad.

Theodore Roosevelt

CHAPTER 2

THE PROFESSIONAL FEES

Absolute took up the assignment for S$18,000.00, with a further contingency amount of S$12,000.00 payable upon achieving the objective of the assignment (i.e. to procure evidence on *Signode's* Managing Director's alleged breaches of his fiduciary duties to legally enable *Signode* to forfeit his gratuity entitlement). *Signode* informed *Absolute* not to prepare any official agreement on the assignment as it wanted secrecy on the matter. *Signode* instructed *Absolute* to send a letter to its lawyers, by referring itself as a "client", without mentioning the objective of the assignment. This letter was sent accordingly to *Signode's* lawyers, *Messrs Ang Tan & Chang* (Appendix 2).

Sometime in March 1998, *Signode* revised the objective of the assignment – which was for *Absolute* to procure evidence for the purpose of effecting a criminal action followed by a civil action against *Signode's* Managing Director. The contingency fee now payable to *Absolute* was pegged to the amount of damages recovered from its Managing Director in the anticipated civil action, capped to a maximum of S$100,000.00. *Signode* subsequently increased this capped amount to S$200,000.00. **A meeting between senior officials of *Signode* and *Absolute* affirming this arrangement was discreetly video recorded.**

*"Our attorney had to skip today's
meeting. He's being sentenced today."*

CHAPTER 3

INVESTIGATIONS & SURVEILLANCE

Absolute cultivated informants within *Signode* to solicit for information/ investigation leads and mounted surveillance on its Managing Director and suspected employees.

After much pain-staking investigation, *Absolute* established the following:

a. *Signode's* Managing Director masterminded the setting up of a rival company mentioned in the earlier mentioned anonymous letter that was sent to *Signode's* headquarters in Chicago.
(It was subsequently established that he was holding the post of a director in this rival company through a proxy.)

b. Several employees colluded with *Signode's* Managing Director and leaked out confidential and privileged information to the rival company that he had set up, resulting in major business losses for *Signode*.

c. A conspiracy between *Signode's* Managing Director and an American to defraud *Signode* of its rightful due from a successfully completed business project.

Signode expressed its satisfaction and informed *Absolute* that it would be consulting its lawyers on the developments.

The law is a sort of hocus-pocus science that smiles in your face while it picks your pocket.

H. L. Mencken

CHAPTER 4

THE DISCARDED INFORMATION

After consulting its lawyers, *Signode* informed *Absolute* that it needed additional information and evidence against its Managing Director. *Absolute* then instructed *Signode* to place an advertisement in the local newspapers to solicit for investigative leads (Appendix 3). It was agreed that the public would be requested to provide information directly to *Signode's* lawyers, who would then re-direct any leads received to *Absolute* so as not to alert anyone that private investigators were involved in the matter.

About three days later, *Signode's* lawyers received a letter from an informant in Malaysia who requested for a handsome reward in exchange for evidence on the following:

- Re-sale of contraband items.
- Conflicting businesses by key managers in Malaysia/Singapore.
- Information leakage to American and European competitors.
- Siphoning of shareholders' funds through connected suppliers.

When *Absolute* wanted to pursue this lead, *Signode* gave strict instructions to discard the information in the said letter, which, according to them, was nonsensical.

It was subsequently established that Signode did not want to pursue this lead as it implicated others, besides its managing director, for professional misconduct. Years later, after the Commercial Affairs Department (CAD) of the Singapore Police Force commenced investigations, the Financial Controller of Signode committed suicide.

7

A lawsuit is a fruit tree planted in a lawyer's garden.

Italian Proverb

CHAPTER 5

THE BLACKMAIL ATTEMPT

When *Absolute* queried *Signode* whether it was going to proceed with whatever action it wanted to take against its Managing Director with the evidence procured thus far at hand, *Signode* claimed that it needed much more than these evidence to ensure a conclusive outcome.

Signode then made an unusual request for *Absolute* to explore "another angle" to close the case on its Managing Director expeditiously. This other angle was for *Absolute* to determine whether *Signode's* Managing Director, a married man, was having relationships with other women.

Absolute decided not to go into this area of investigations when it became apparent that *Signode* wanted to blackmail its Managing Director if he was having any extra-marital activities. *Absolute* then informed *Signode* that its investigations would be confined to procure evidence on breaches of the fiduciary duties of its Managing Director and not any extra-marital matters.

"My client pleads not guilty, your
honor, just for the sake of
argument."

CHAPTER 6

INTERNAL INVESTIGATION

Absolute could not communicate directly with *Signode's* employees (refer to Chapter 2, paragraph 1) as its appointment was secret. Hence, *Absolute* instructed *Signode* to conduct an internal investigation by requesting its employees to sign statutory declarations respectively before a Commissioner for Oaths that they had not engaged in any activities against the interest of the company. *Absolute* was quite certain the guilty employees would not sign this declaration for fear of criminal charges being instituted against them for false declaration.

After the statutory declaration exercise was completed, *Signode* reported to *Absolute* that its Managing Director and two other staff had refused to sign the statutory declaration. **Signode expressed its satisfaction on the outcome of the exercise as the suspicion on its Managing Director's disloyalty was confirmed.** *Absolute* then instructed *Signode* to form an investigation panel and interview certain people, with the information/ evidence at hand, to obtain their confirmed testimonies on the actions of *Signode's* Managing Director's that would conclusively prove that he had breached his fiduciary duties.

An investigation panel was formed, comprising *Signode's* lawyer, *Juliet Ang* and the Executive Director & General Manager of *Signode's* related company in Hong Kong, *William Yao*. After hearing the interviewees, **the investigation panel came to an "inescapable" conclusion that the actions of *Signode's* Managing Director were**

irregular and not consistent with those expected of the Chief Executive Officer of a company (Appendix 4 – this report is not displayed in its entirety to protect the identities of those who had testified in the internal investigation).

Following the investigation panel's report, *Signode* suspended its Managing Director from his duties. After receiving the suspension notice, *Signode's* Managing Director made a private settlement offer to forgo his gratuity entitlement in consideration of all claims/actions against him to be dropped. The other employees whom *Absolute* had established of having colluded with him tendered in their resignations immediately.

CHAPTER 7

PRIVATE SETTLEMENT

Signode instructed *Absolute* to discontinue its investigations in view of its Managing Director's offer of a private settlement. *Absolute* expressed its concern over *Signode's* interest in wanting to consider this offer as its contingency fee was pegged up to S$200,000.00 of the amount *Signode* would gain in the anticipated civil action against its managing director. *Signode* informed *Absolute* that it was advised by its lawyers to accept the private settlement offer as it would be futile to proceed with any civil action against its Managing Director because of a peculiar clause in his employment agreement that would give him double the gratuity amount if he were to be terminated. The following is the extract from his Employment Agreement that was highlighted by *Signode*:

> "...*the Company shall, upon such termination pay forthwith to the Managing Director the following termination benefits.... For every year of employment of the Managing Director with the Company, two (2) months of the Managing Director's monthly remuneration* ..."

Absolute then pointed out that this clause could be legally voided as its Managing Director had committed a criminal offence under the Company's Act for breaching his fiduciary duties. *Signode's* lawyers agreed but said in that instance, its Managing Director would only be fined a maximum of $5,000.00 and yet could still claim his gratuity by using another clause found in another document, namely his Deed of Gratuity, which allowed him to receive his gratuity in the event of the termination of his employment on any grounds whatsoever. The following is the extract from his Deed of Gratuity that was highlighted by *Signode*:

> "...the Company hereby agrees and undertakes to, upon the termination of the Managing Director's employment on any grounds whatsoever, including the resignation of the Managing Director, pay forthwith to the Managing Director a total sum being an amount equivalent aggregate of one (1) month of the Managing Director's monthly remuneration ....from August 1, 1987."

***Signode* then assured *Absolute* that its contingency fees of S$200,000.00 (less the S$18,000.00 received earlier in two tranches) would still be payable if its Managing Director's private settlement offer went through successfully.** *Absolute* then relented as it was in the best interest of all parties to see through the private settlement.

CHAPTER 8

HICCUPS IN THE PRIVATE SETTLEMENT

The private settlement negotiations between *Signode* and its Managing Director did not go as smoothly as anticipated. *Signode's* requirement in the private settlement that its Managing Director bear the legal costs of engaging the Commissioner For Oaths (refer to Chapter 6) was rejected by him, as he felt that it was unfair to penalize him to bear this cost as he did not sign any statutory declaration before the said commissioner. *Signode*, on the other hand, rejected its Managing Director's request for an undertaking not to take out any claims/action against all the staff who had colluded with him.

After some wrangling, *Signode's* Managing Director caved in to all the stringent terms imposed by *Signode*, which included the following:

a. withdrawal of his request for Signode's undertaking that no claims/ action would be taken against all the staff who had colluded with him;

b. withdrawal of his request not to pay for the legal costs incurred in engaging the Commissioner For Oaths;

c. to pay Signode its legal costs on a solicitor/client basis for an amount in the region of $60,000.00.

The private settlement finally ended to the satisfaction of *Signode*. *Signode* congratulated *Absolute* for having carried out its assignment successfully and gave an assurance that the balance of its professional fees of $182,000.00 ($200,000 less $18,000 given earlier in two tranches) would be settled in due course.

*The only way you can beat the lawyers is
to die with nothing.*

Will Rogers

CHAPTER 9

THE BOMBSHELL

Whilst waiting patiently to receive its outstanding fees, **Signode** dropped a bombshell on **Absolute.** It claimed that its shareholders were against paying the outstanding amount to **Absolute,** since no civil action was taken against its Managing Director, and offered an ex-gratia amount of $30,000.00 instead. *Absolute* rejected the offer and informed *Signode* that it would seek legal redress. *Signode* then persuaded *Absolute* to accept the S$30,000.00 from its lawyers, and it would subsequently endeavour to settle the difference through another special business arrangement. Hence, *Absolute* accepted *Signode's* proposal to accept S$30,000.00 from its lawyers, with the balance amount settled through another business arrangement.

Subsequently, *Absolute* sent a courier to *Signode's* lawyers' office to collect the cheque for S$30,000.00. Upon the courier's arrival, *Signode's* lawyers telephoned *Absolute* and requested for an official invoice, before it could release the cheque to the courier. *Absolute* then consulted *Signode* on the necessity of invoicing, as it never invoiced them for the $18,000.00 received earlier in two tranches from Signode's lawyers. *Signode* informed *Absolute* to comply with its lawyers' request to give a supporting invoice for the $30,000.00, and for the $18,000.00 received earlier – as both these amounts were paid out through the legal firm and needed to be accounted for. *Signode* then assured *Absolute* the balance amount would be paid directly by *Signode* through a special business arrangement without involving its lawyers.

Absolute obliged accordingly and looked forward to this special business arrangement to receive the balance payment of its professional fees, which now stood at $152,000.00 ($200,000.00 less $18,000.00 received earlier in two tranches and the latest $30,000.00, the so-called ex-gratia amount given by the shareholders of *Signode* to *Absolute*, since no civil action was taken against its Managing Director).

CHAPTER 10

A SPECIAL BUSINESS ARRANGEMENT

The special business arrangement through which *Absolute* would receive its balance fees of $152,000.00 was basically through trading, i.e., *Absolute* would purchase steel strapping of specifications stipulated by *Signode* and re-sell them to *Signode* at a profit margin to recover its outstanding fees of $152,000.00.

After receiving the steel strapping specifications from *Signode* (Appendix 5), *Absolute* made numerous trade enquiries through its affiliated company, *Omnix International Pte Ltd* (Appendix 6). There were responses to the said trade enquiries from steel manufacturers (Appendix 7), but none of them were acceptable to *Signode*.

After making more futile trade enquiries, *Absolute* realized it was going on a wild goose chase to purchase something it would not be able to do so within the satisfaction of *Signode*. Subsequently, *Absolute* informed *Signode* that if it did not settle the outstanding professional fees, it would resort to legal action. **Signode then gave a veiled threat to Absolute that it would jeopardize itself if the matter went to Court as its covert operations in the assignment undertaken would be challenged and made public.**

"The signatures are from my
attorneys for the malpractice suit."

CHAPTER 11

LEGAL REDRESS

Absolute took its first legal action against *Signode* in October 1998 at the Subordinate Court. *Signode* was represented by *Messrs L. S. Tan & Company* whilst *Absolute* by *Messrs Ang & Lee*.

In its Defence, **Signode falsely claimed the evidence procured by Absolute were *insufficient* to warrant any criminal/civil proceedings against its Managing Director** and hence, *Absolute* did not deserve more than the S$18,000.00 it had received in two tranches when it took up the assignment. *Signode* stated an additional amount of S$30,000.00 was given on an ex-gratia basis and *Absolute* had acknowledged it as the full and final settlement of its dues.

Signode submitted to the Court a photocopy of its lawyers' cheque (Appendix 8) which had the words "… in full and final settlement" and the signature of the person who collected the cheque. This was the first time *Absolute* sighted this document and objected to it being admitted as evidence as the person who had collected the cheque was a courier and not an employee of *Absolute*. The courier had merely signed on the photocopied cheque to acknowledge receipt – a common practice carried out by couriers who collect documents for their clients.

During the course of the legal action, *Absolute* realized that a crucial document, i.e. the letter from the informant in Malaysia (refer to Chapter 4, paragraph 2) was not submitted to the Court. Hence, *Absolute's* lawyers wrote to *Signode's* lawyers for this copy to be submitted as evidence – as *Absolute* wanted to highlight to the Court that its investigative efforts were not taken seriously by *Signode*. **When *Signode* feigned ignorance on this particular evidence, *Absolute* applied to the Court to compel *Signode* to produce this letter** (Appendix 9). *Signode* subsequently produced the said letter (Appendix 10).

When the matter came to trial, *Absolute* requested the Court to annul the private settlement between *Signode* and its Managing Director for the evidence that it had procured to be used against him in a legal action. Midway during the trial, the Court adjourned the matter and requested lawyers from both parties to give their submissions as the Court considered *Absolute's* position to compel compulsory legal action without the possibility of a private settlement was against public policy. **The Court then dismissed *Absolute* action summarily on this point of law (without examining the evidence that *Absolute* had procured against Signode's managing director).**

Absolute appealed against the dismissal in July 1999 at the High Court. *Signode* was represented by *Messrs Tan & Koh Partnership* whilst *Absolute* by *Messrs Tan Rajah & Cheah*. The High Court upheld the decision of the Subordinate Court, i.e. that it was against public policy to compel compulsory legal action without the possibility of a settlement.

When *Absolute* expressed its disappointment on the High Court's decision, *Messrs Tan Rajah & Cheah* highlighted that its "Statement of Claim" filed originally at the Subordinate Court was defective and it could take out a professional negligence claim against its previous lawyers. *Messrs Tan Rajah & Cheah* added that they could not act for *Absolute* in the said negligence claim due to a conflict of interest (as they had represented *Absolute* in the appeal) but could do so for in a fresh claim against *Signode*, upon conclusion of the negligence claim.

Absolute appointed *Messrs Jacob Mansur & Pillai* in its negligence claim against its previous lawyers, *Messrs Ang & Lee*, who was represented by *Messrs Kenneth Tan Partnership*. The action was subsequently discontinued after an "Offer to Settle" the matter was accepted by *Absolute*. Thereafter, when *Absolute* conferred with *Messrs Tan Rajah & Cheah* on a fresh claim against *Signode*, it was advised to go directly to *Signode* to explore an amicable settlement. If this was unsuccessful, fresh proceedings could ensue.

CHAPTER 12

EXPLORATION FOR AN AMICABLE SETTLEMENT

When *Absolute* approached *Signode* to explore an amicable settlement, *Signode's* General Manager, *Toh Boon Leng* claimed he was unaware of any outstanding fees due to *Absolute* as the key officers who had engaged *Absolute* were no longer with the company. One of them had committed suicide whilst under investigation by the police for embezzlement and the other had resigned.

As the credibility of the old management who had engaged the services of *Absolute* was in doubt, *Toh Boon Leng* informed *Absolute* that it was unnecessary to proceed with any fresh proceedings to recover its outstanding fees if its new management can be convinced of this debt. **He further added that *Signode* was a reputable Fortune 500 Company worth millions of dollars and it would have no problem paying *Absolute* its dues if it was genuine.**

Toh Boon Leng then informed *Absolute* to contact *Andrew Beeson* from Australia who was in charge of the *Signode's* affairs in Singapore. After discussion with *Andrew Beeson*, it was agreed that *Signode* would appoint its own consultant to carry out investigations and advise them whether *Absolute's* claim for its outstanding fees of S$152,000.00 was genuine – and if so, settle the said amount accordingly.

Be frank and explicit with your lawyer. It is his business to confuse the issue afterwards.

Anonymous

CHAPTER 13

THE INTERNATIONAL CONSULTANT

May 2002

Signode appointed *Kroll Inc*, an international risk consulting company (www.kroll.com), to carry out investigations for the purpose of advising *Signode* as to whether the alleged sum of $152,000.00 was outstanding to *Absolute* for an assignment undertaken in March 1998.

Kroll is no ordinary company. It is the world's leading business risk consultancy, with more than 30 years' experience. With offices in 55 cities in the US and abroad, *Kroll* can conduct in-depth investigations, scrutinize accounting practices, financial documents, gather and filter electronic evidence for attorneys, recover lost or damaged data from computers and servers, etc. *Kroll's* clients include many of the world's largest and most prestigious corporations, law firms, academic institutions, non-profit organizations, sovereign governments, government agencies, high net-worth individuals, entertainers and celebrities

Absolute cooperated fully with *Kroll* during its investigations. Confidential files and evidence were scrutinized by *Kroll* and officers from *Absolute* were interrogated. After completing its task, **Kroll** **expressed its satisfaction over the alleged outstanding amount of $152,000.00 due to *Absolute* and praised the private investigation agency's professional prowess.**

When *Absolute* requested for a letter attesting to this, *Kroll* said that it was not proper to do so as they were engaged by *Signode* and had to liaise with them. **Kroll, nevertheless, said that it would be submitting its report to *Signode* and *Absolute* should be receiving its rightful dues in time.**

CHAPTER 14

THE LEGAL WALTZ

December 2002
About 8 months passed since *Kroll* had completed its appointed task for *Signode* and confirmed that the outstanding sum of $152,000.00 due to *Absolute* was bona fide. When there was no response, *Absolute* instructed its lawyers, *Messrs Tan Rajah & Cheah* to send a letter to *Signode* (Appendix 11) highlighting the following:

a.   *Absolute's* resort to seek legal redress through the courts for its rightful dues was thwarted by a defective action, which was subsequently addressed through a professional negligence claim against its previous lawyers.

b.   **Absolute had handed over various documents to *Signode's* consultant, *Kroll* and given their full cooperation in order for *Kroll* to advise *Signode* on the matter.**

c.   *Absolute* was disappointed that nothing had evolved after *Kroll's* services were engaged.

d.   ***Signode's* leading witness had suppressed crucial evidence and *Absolute* would seek to impeach this witness should fresh proceedings be taken against *Signode*.**

e.   *Absolute* was prepared to work out an amicable settlement to resolve the matter expeditiously in lieu of fresh proceedings against *Signode*.

April 2003

When about three months went by without any response from *Signode* to the earlier mentioned letter, *Absolute* sought the help of *Andrew Beeson,* who replied that he had handed over the said letter from *Messrs Tan Rajah & Cheah* to *Signode's* lawyers in Singapore and to its head office in Chicago (Appendix 12).

Absolute also contacted *Kroll* and informed them it would proceed with fresh proceedings against *Signode* as there was nothing happening. **Kroll responded immediately and advised Absolute to resolve the matter amicably and not resort to any court action.**

Signode finally responded through its lawyers, *Messrs David Lim & Partners* (Appendix 13) on 24 Apr 2003 and requested for more time, without addressing any of the issues raised.

March 2005

The matter dragged on further for another two years. In March 2005, *Messrs Tan Rajah & Cheah* requested *Messrs David Lim & Partners* for their response whether *Signode* was willing to consider an amicable settlement on the outstanding professional fees, failing which *Absolute* had to resort to legal action. *Messrs David Lim & Partners* requested for more time as their client was based in the United States (Appendix 14).

April 2005

In April 2005, *Messrs Tan Rajah & Cheah* proposed a meeting between all parties to work out a resolution. *Messrs David Lim & Partners* responded that *Signode* would not be attending the meeting but was open to a written proposal from *Absolute* for its consideration (Appendix 15). *Messrs Tan Rajah & Cheah* responded accordingly (Appendix 16), highlighting *Absolute's* offer to forgo its legal costs and interest incurred and accept only its outstanding professional fees of $152,000.00 as full and final settlement in the matter.

June 2005

When *Messrs David Lim & Partners* did not respond to the written proposal sent by *Messrs Tan Rajah & Cheah, Absolute* felt it was pointless to engage in further legal diplomacy as it was heading nowhere and decided to proceed with a fresh action against *Signode.* On receiving information that *Messrs Tan Rajah & Cheah* were involved in other urgent matters and may not have the time to handle its case, *Absolute* decided to appoint *Messrs Riaz, Ian Chang & Pat Quah* to take over the matter – to which *Messrs Tan Rajah & Cheah* stated that it had no objections (Appendix 17).

Messrs Riaz, Ian Chang & Pat Quah wrote to *Messrs David Lim & Partners* on 14 Jun 2005 (Appendix 18), informing them they had taken over the conduct of the matter from *Messrs Tan Rajah & Cheah* and repeated the proposal outlined in the earlier mentioned letter of *Messrs Tan Rajah & Cheah* to resolve the matter expeditiously.

When it became apparent that *Signode* did not want to resolve the matter amicably, *Absolute* discharged *Messrs Riaz Ian Chang & Pat Quah*, as the ambit of their appointment in terms of legal costs was to secure an amicable settlement. To re-appoint *Messrs Riaz, Ian Chang & Pat Quah* for the purpose of commencing legal action against *Signode* proved costly for *Absolute*. One of the directors of *Absolute*, a former police officer, was then recommended by an acquaintance to *Messrs Vijay & Company*, a law firm managed by *Vijay Kumar*, a dedicated volunteer Senior Police Officer with a benevolent heart, to handle the matter.

I used to be a lawyer, but now I am a reformed character.

Woodrow Wilson

CHAPTER 15

BACK TO COURT

November 2005

In November 2005, *Absolute* commenced fresh proceedings against *Signode* at the Subordinate Court. *Signode* was represented by *Messrs David Lim & Partners* whilst *Absolute* by *Messrs Vijay & Company*.

The crux of the legal argument in this action was on the oral agreement between *Signode* and *Absolute* to allow *Signode's* consultant, namely *Kroll*, to carry out investigations whether *Absolute's* claim for its outstanding professional fees of $152,000.00 was bona fide; and if so, *Signode* would stand to be advised by *Kroll* to settle the amount accordingly.

Signode falsely stated in a court document that the oral agreement involving Kroll to investigate Absolute's claim for its outstanding professional fees did not exist and was made up by Absolute (Appendix 19). Conversely, in a separate court document, *Signode* admitted appointing *Kroll* to investigate *Absolute's* claim but refused to make known the findings of *Kroll*, stating that the work carried out by *Kroll* was work done in contemplation of legal proceedings and therefore the information was privileged (Appendix 20). **The refusal by Signode to produce Kroll's findings speaks volume**.

Messrs David Lim & Partners falsely stated in a court document that Absolute had concocted the agreement with Signode to appoint Kroll in order to justify its right to commence

fresh legal proceedings against Signode (Appendix 21). *Messrs David Lim & Partners* further submitted that this agreement was a creation of *Absolute* as it was not mentioned in its earlier letters of demand, namely from *Messrs Tan Rajah & Cheah* (Appendix 11) and *Messrs Riaz, Ian Chang and Pat Quah* (Appendix 18) to *Signode*.

As a matter of fact, the said letters were not letters of demand but letters of request for an amicable settlement of the outstanding professional fees due to *Absolute*. Most importantly, there was mention of *Kroll* being engaged by *Signode* in one of these letters (Appendix 11, paragraph 4). In the said letter, *Messrs Tan Rajah & Cheah* highlighted that *Signode* had engaged the services of *Kroll* for advice on the matter and *Absolute* had given its cooperation accordingly. **This conclusively proved that there was an arrangement between *Signode* and *Absolute* which involved *Kroll* in relation to the outstanding professional fees.**

Signode applied to the Court for a summary dismissal of *Absolute's* claim, which would deny the opportunity of a proper hearing to examine the issues in question. *Messrs Vijay & Company* objected to this application, stating **the allegation that *Absolute* had concocted the agreement involving *Kroll* was serious and imputed fraud. *Messrs Vijay & Company* argued that this was an issue of fact, which has to be determined by evidence during a proper hearing; where witnesses would be called to testify (especially *Kroll*, for its conclusive testimony on its findings).**

Messrs David Lim & Partners objected to having a proper hearing and pursued for a summary judgment in chambers as its legal manoeuvre was not to dispute the facts on the appointment of *Kroll* to ascertain whether *Absolute's* claim was bona fide (as this would be would mean that *Kroll* would be called to testify and submit its findings) but to amplify 3 points of law before the Learned Registrar of the Court.

Messrs David Lim & Partners argued that even if the agreement involving *Kroll* was genuine, it was invalid and unenforceable on the ground that there was an *"absence of consideration"* (1st point of law). The next argument was the agreement involving *Kroll* was based on a debt that was owing latest by 13 October 1998 and more than six years had passed since Absolute filed its claim for the said debt, and cannot pursue further as it was *"time-barred"* (2nd point of law). The final argument was that since *Absolute's* first claim was dismissed in 1998, it could no longer commence any proceedings against *Signode* for the recovery of any debt prior to 13 October 1998 and in doing so was an abuse of process under the *extended doctrine of res judicata* (3rd point of law).

Messrs Vijay & Company argued it was inappropriate to claim that there was an "absence of consideration" in the agreement involving *Kroll*, as the consideration was present in the form of *forebearance to sue* (Appendix 22). On the issue of *time-bar,* the agreement involving Kroll was entered in March 2002 and *Absolute* had filed its claim in November 2005 (less than six years); *Absolute's* cause of action arose after *Kroll* had completed its investigations and reported the findings to *Signode* and when subsequently *Signode* failed to make good the outstanding fees owing to *Absolute*, as agreed if *Kroll* was satisfied that the said amount was rightfully due to *Absolute*. As for the point of law on the "extended doctrine of res judicata", *Messrs Vijay & Company argued* that it did not apply to the particular circumstances of *Absolute's* claim.

The Learned Registrar ruled that the cause of action, in this case, was founded on the compromise agreement (involving *Kroll*). The consideration of "forbearance to sue" was linked to *Absolute's* first claim in 1998, which no longer exists, and to latch on to that as a course of action would both be "res judicata" in the extended sense and an abuse of process to get around the time bar. Hence, the said agreement lacked the basis of that consideration and therefore, could not be a valid contract (Appendix 23).

After the Court dismissed *Absolute's* claim, *Absolute* sought the help of the *Commercial Affairs Department* (CAD) of the *Singapore Police Force* (Appendix 24) to discredit *Signode's* evidence in Court, in preparation for an appeal against the dismissal of *Absolute's* claim by the Learned Registrar. The CAD responded they were unable to assist *Absolute* in the matter as the information arising from their investigations was strictly confidential (Appendix 25). *Absolute's* director then went personally to CAD to appeal for a reconsideration of its position as there had been a travesty of justice and requested for a testimony from the investigating officer in *Signode's* matter so that it could be tendered as evidence in its appeal. CAD maintained its position but informed the Director that *Absolute* could make an application to the Court to subpoena the investigating officer on the matter when a trial is ordered for the said appeal.

Absolute appealed against the Learned Registrar's decision in the Subordinate Courts. *Messrs Vijay & Company's* further arguments for *Absolute* are found in Appendix 26. Unfortunately for *Absolute*, the earlier ruling by the Learned Registrar was upheld. **This denied a proper hearing for *Absolute* that would have seen testimonies from witnesses, especially from *Kroll*, that it was firmly established that *Signode* received satisfactory professional services from *Absolute* and hence was duty-bound to pay the alleged outstanding professional fees accordingly.**

The only option available now for *Absolute* was to appeal to the High Court. However, after having been drained of its financial resources, this was not viable.

CHAPTER 16

THE BOOK THAT WAS NEVER PUBLISHED

October 2006

As *Absolute* was no longer in a position to seek legal redress to recover its rightful dues, it decided to close the matter. However, one of *Absolute's* directors, namely *Gilbert Pereira*, decided to pursue it on his personal capacity through a publication of a book titled DISMISSED WITHOUT TRIAL. He hoped for this book to draw attention from the right people who would be able to persuade the principal company of *Signode*, namely *Illinois Tool Works Inc (ITW)* to use the gentleman's approach to resolve the outstanding sum due to *Absolute*.

Gilbert wrote to *Messrs David Lim & Partners* on 26 Oct 2006 on the pending publication of DISMISSED WITHOUT TRIAL. This letter (Appendix 27) highlighted **the fact that *Absolute's* claim for its outstanding professional fees was struck off by the Court on a point of law and not on the fact this amount was rightfully owing by *Signode*.** The letter also gave *Signode* the opportunity to review its contents before publication, with an assurance to make the necessary amendments to objectionable points raised that cannot be justified. When *Messrs David Lim & Partners* did not respond to this letter, Gilbert wrote directly to *Signode* on 7 Nov 2006 on the same subject matter.

On 12 Dec 2006, *Messrs David Lim & Partners* responded to the earlier mentioned letter and stated that the publication material could be defamatory and in contempt of Court – and would take any steps necessary against *Gilbert* through legal action and the relevant authorities in Singapore (Appendix 28).

Gilbert then sought legal advice whether the book was defamatory and in contempt of Court. He was informed that the contents of the book may be defamatory if they were inaccurate or cannot be substantiated when challenged. Hence, he was advised to offer *Messrs David Lim & Partners* and their clients an opportunity to raise objections to its contents for the purpose of amending them if these objections were valid. As for the book being in contempt of Court, it was due to its title, DISMISSED WITHOUT TRIAL – as there was a trial in its first legal action against *Signode*, which was suspended midway that resulted in a summary judgment against *Absolute* on a point of law (refer to Chapter 11, paragraph 4). *Gilbert* then decided to shelf this book project.

CHAPTER 17

THE BOOK THAT WAS PUBLISHED

In order to recover the losses incurred through the decade in the legal battle between *Absolute* and *Signode*, *Gilbert* decided to publish another book that he was certain would not invite any lawsuits for defamation or contempt of Court — as the contents revolved around lawyers and courtroom incidents within a humorous setting. Its title, FACTUALLY YES, LEGALLY NO! was derived from the fact that *Signode* owed *Absolute* its outstanding fees of $152,000.00 but legally, *Absolute* could not claim this amount! *The Straits Times* reviewed this book on September 11, 2008 (Appendix 29).

A lawyer with a briefcase can steal more than a thousand men with guns

Mario Puzo

CHAPTER 18

THE PERSONAL APPEAL AND ITS DEVELOPMENTS

As the book sales were not enough to recover the losses, *Gilbert* decided to appeal for help from the principal company of *Signode*, namely *Illinois Tool Works Inc (ITW Inc)*.

On 7 Jan 2009, **Gilbert** approached **Andre Accad**, the **Managing Director of ITW Singapore for help; who then referred the matter to his corporate office in Illinois, USA. Subsequently, *James Wooten*, the Senior Vice-President, General Counsel and Secretary of *ITW Inc* contacted *Gilbert* for more details on the matter.**

On 16 Jan 2009, *Gilbert* wrote to *James Wooten* (Appendix 30) and attached the facts of the case involving *Absolute* and *Signode*. The appendices (Evidence File) were left out as they were voluminous and most importantly had privileged and confidential information amongst them. *Gilbert* proposed to allow *Andre Accad* to scrutinize the appendices in Singapore, on *James Wooten's* behalf. Alternatively, *Gilbert* offered to fly to USA with the documents. There was no response to both offers.

On 22 Jan 2009, *Gilbert* wrote to *James Wooten* (Appendix 31) via another email address as he was concerned the earlier email may not have gone through – since there was no response. *James Wooten* replied immediately, confirming receipt of *Gilbert's* earlier email and that he was reviewing the facts of the case (without the appendices) and would respond shortly (Appendix 32).

On 27 Feb 2009, *Gilbert* wrote to *James Wooten* (Appendix 33) and expressed his disappointment that five weeks had passed by without his communication on the matter, especially that no request was made for the appendices (Evidence File) to be examined – as no justifiable conclusion can be made without this examination. *Gilbert* then proposed either for the *US Embassy in Singapore* to examine the appendices or for *Andre Accad* to do so on behalf of *James Wooten.*

On 2 Mar 2009, *James Wooten* replied (Appendix 34), apologizing for the delay in response and at the same time gave baseless reasons (parroting *Messrs David Lim & Partners'* position in the matter) for not wanting to honour *Absolute's* claim.

James Wooten's groundless reasons are reproduced below, with *Gilbert's* response to him in italics:

a. "After reviewing the materials you submitted, we have concluded that you are seeking payment of $152,000.00 for which there is almost no support."

The support is found in my Evidence File (the appendices) – which contains privileged and confidential information in the form of documents, video recordings of meetings and recordings of telephone conversations. You have yet to accept my offer to have this file reviewed.

b. "While you reference numerous attachments in support of or claim, it is apparent you do not have documentation supporting the alleged increase in the contingency fee to $200,000.00 or that the increased contingency fee would be paid without a successful civil action..."

You are repeating what Signode told me in the year 2002 that there is no documentation to support our claim. It is precisely for this reason that Signode appointed Kroll (the world's leading consulting company) to investigate and advise whether it should honour our claim as there was no proper documentation.

c. "Moreover, despite having filed three (3) legal actions against Signode, no court has found merit in your claims."

It is an understatement to say in all our 3 legal actions the Court found no merit in our claims. Please examine the real issues that were deliberated by the Court. None of the judges said we were making a false claim. The

Court (in all 3 actions) took issue on the legal enforceability of the contract involving the contingency fees and not on its factuality.

d.   "Unfortunately, we have no personal knowledge of any of the facts surrounding your claim and, therefore, can only judge your claim based upon the facts you have provided."

This is a similar comment made by Signode back in 2002, which led to my company entering into an agreement to allow Kroll to look into our confidential working files and evidence to determine the facts of our claim with the view of resolving the matter out-of-court. **Thereafter, Signode did the dishonourable thing by refusing to honor the findings of Kroll and resorted to legalities (with the help of Messrs David Lim & Partners) to avoid paying us our rightful dues.**

e.   "We regret to inform you that the facts you have presented do not provide sufficient basis to pay your claim."

Precisely for this reason, I am humbly requesting that you have my Evidence File reviewed. If you cannot come to Singapore to do this, please appoint Andrew Acaad to do so on our behalf. Andrew is the managing director of ITW Singapore and can be trusted with the privileged and confidential information contained in my Evidence File.

Subsequently, **Gilbert** forwarded to **James Wooten** video footages of a meeting (discreetly recorded) where high-ranking officers from **Signode** acknowledged the outstanding fees payable to **Absolute** and blamed their lawyers for not being firm in taking action against the managing director for breaching his fiduciary duties. These recordings were brushed aside as not being conclusive and *James Wooten*, having full knowledge of *Kroll's* findings was very cautious in not making any reference to them in any of his correspondence with *Gilbert*.

Only painters and lawyers can change white to black.

Japanese Proverb

CHAPTER 19

THE PUBLIC APPEAL AND ITS DEVELOPMENTS

As all personal attempts by *Gilbert* to recover the rightful dues of *Absolute* from *Signode* were thwarted through corporate deception by *Signode* and its legal battalion, *Gilbert* decided to go public and appeal on the moral conscience of *David Speer*, the CEO of *ITW Inc.* in Illinois, Chicago to do the gentlemanly thing, i.e. instruct *Signode* to honour its dues to *Absolute*. Hence, *Gilbert* went forward to make preparations to issue a press release and also conduct a petition letter-signing event at The Speakers' Corner to garner support from the public.

Whilst preparing to issue a press release, *Gilbert* was advised to offer concerned parties the opportunity to raise objections to any part of the contents of his press statement that may need to be amended or withdrawn. Hence, *Gilbert* offered this opportunity to all of them by way of a letter dated 23 Jun 2009 (Appendix 35). **Only *ITW Singapore*, responded by stating it did not have any clues about the whole matter** (Appendix 36). **This response was rather odd, especially when *ITW Singapore* had *directed* Gilbert to its corporate office in USA when it first came to know of the details on the outstanding professional fees due to Absolute by Signode** (refer to Chapter 18, paragraph 2).

Approval was granted to *Gilbert* by the authorities to conduct his petition letter-signing event at The Speakers' Corner on 31 July 2009. In order to draw the right target audience, *Gilbert* prepared an invitation letter to the public (Appendix 37) to be distributed around the area of the said event. About two weeks prior to this event, *Gilbert* was advised by well-meaning friends to cancel it if its objective (i.e. to persuade *David Speer*, CEO of *ITW Inc* to honour the findings of *Kroll* on Absolute's claim) can be achieved through the intervention of the parties concerned. Hence, on 17 Jul 2009, *Gilbert* wrote to these parties on an individual basis (Appendix 38) on the upcoming petition letter-signing event at The Speakers' Corner. It was expressed in this letter that if the objective of the said event could be achieved through their intervention, the event would be cancelled. Enclosed with the said letter was the earlier mentioned invitation letter to the public for the parties to raise objections to any part(s) therein for amendments to be done, if necessary.

Since there was no response from any parties to the earlier mentioned letter, *Gilbert* went ahead with his petition letter-signing event at the Speakers' Corner on 31 Jul 2009. The following day, when *Gilbert* was accessing his emails, he came across an email from *Suresh Damodara*, a lawyer from *Messrs David Lim & Partners* (Appendix 39) with attachments. The first attachment (Appendix 39.1) was a "cease and desist" letter, accusing *Gilbert* of defamation and extortion, among other things. **It threatened him that *Signode* and *Messrs David Lim & Partners* would proceed to take legal action if he did not carry out the following within 24 hours:**

a.   Apologize in writing in a format agreeable to *Signode* and *Messrs David Lim & Partners;*

b.   Cease and desist from all threatened and future conduct and to provide a written undertaking in this regard in a format agreeable to *Signode* and *Messrs David Lim & Partners;*

c.   Provide an undertaking to pay damages to *Signode* and *Messrs David Lim & Partners.*

The second attachment to the earlier mentioned email (Appendix 39.2) was a duplicate copy of *Gilbert's* letter dated 17 Jul 2009 to various parties concerned for their intervention to abort the petition letter-signing event at The Speakers' Corner on 31 Jul 2009. **It is rather strange that *Messrs David Lim & Partners*, having acknowledged receiving this letter on 20 Jul 2009, chose to respond on the day of the event at the eleventh hour.**

Gilbert immediately responded to *Suresh Damodara* and asked him the relevance of his email as the event at The Speakers' Corner was already over; which was sent less than 2 hours before the event and the hard copy couriered to *Gilbert's* office about an hour later – when *Gilbert* was already on his way to The Speakers' Corner.

Gilbert denied the allegations stated by *Suresh Damodara* in his letter and informed him that the threatened legal action was intimidating and tantamount to extorting from *Gilbert* an apology and damages for something that he had not done and never intended to do (Appendix 40). **If *Messrs David Lim & Partners* and *Signode* were serious about their position that *Gilbert* had resorted to defamation and extortion (which is a criminal offense), they could have applied to the relevant authorities to cancel the petition letter-signing event at The Speakers' Corner, as they were informed of this event about a month earlier.**

Resorting to threaten *Gilbert* at the umpteenth hour of the event by an established law firm as *Messrs David Lim & Partners*, and knowing especially that this threat would not reach *Gilbert* in time made no sense then. On hindsight, this could had been done deliberately to allow *Gilbert* to make his speech at The Speakers' Corner and hopefully utter *defamatory* remarks – which would allow *Signode* and *Messrs David Lim & Partners* to proceed with legal action against him – as there were private investigators from another agency present at The Speakers' Corner recording his speech. However, *Gilbert* was cautious and ensured his speech was based on facts that can be substantiated and hence, "defamatory proof".

A formal letter was sent to *Messrs David Lim & Partners* by *Gilbert* on 3 Aug 2009 (Appendix 41) emphasizing the following:

a.   the allegation that *Gilbert* had perpetrated defamatory remarks for the single purpose of extorting from *Signode* and *Messrs David Lim & Partners* for the sum of $152,000.00 was denied;

b.   the threatened legal action by *Messrs David Lim & Partners'* was intimidating and tantamount to extorting from *Gilbert* an apology and damages for something that he had not done and never intended to do;

c.   all concerned parties were given ample time to raise objections on the event at The Speakers' Corner but chose to do so at the last hour (which resulted in the notice being received by *Gilbert* after the event was over).

In the same letter, *Gilbert* requested for a meeting to produce proof that whatever remarks made by him were not defamatory as they were based on factual evidence. When there was no response to this letter for over a month, Gilbert contacted *Messrs David Lim & Partners* and was told that *Suresh Damodara*, and the lawyers who had previously handled *Absolute's* matter, namely *Sunil Gil* and *Leonard Hazra* had resigned and the "boss", *David Lim* was personally handling the file.

Gilbert forwarded his petition letter (Appendix 42) that culminated from his earlier mentioned public appeal at The Speakers' Corner to *David Speer*, CEO of *ITW Inc*, requesting him to carry out the following:

a.　to ascertain the facts of the matter, especially whether the appointment of *Kroll* to carry out investigations and advise *Signode* on the validity of *Absolute's* claim was genuine – with the understanding that if this was so, *Absolute* was to receive its rightful dues;

b.　**to investigate why *Messrs David Lim & Partners*, after doing its due diligence, brazenly gave false submission to the Court** that *Absolute* had concocted the agreement involving *Kroll*.

When *David Speer* did not respond to the said petition letter, *Gilbert* made several unsuccessful attempts to reach him by telephone. On 1 Sep 2009, *Gilbert* received an email from *James Wooten* stating they have considered the matter closed and will not be making any payments whatsoever (Appendix 43).

With all the betrayals and denials, *Gilbert* conceded that it would be a waste of time convincing *David Speer* or *James Wooten* that the money owing to *Absolute* was genuine because their insincerity was reflected in their attitude in not getting *Kroll* to clarify *Absolute's* assertion that it was engaged by *Signode* to investigate whether *Absolute's* claim for its outstanding professional fees of $152,000.00 was genuine – **because Kroll, being a honourable world-renowned company would definitely reveal the truth that had been conveniently swept under the carpet through corporate deception.**

CHAPTER 20

THE FINAL CURTAIN

After *Gilbert's* speech at The Speakers' Corner on 31 July 2009 was featured in YouTube, he received numerous calls, urging him to come up with a revised edition of his earlier book titled FACTUALLY YES, LEGALLY NO! He was encouraged to include details on the events that occurred, with supporting documents. Some proposed a different title to reflect the unscrupulous behaviour of the "big boys." The general opinion was a book with all the intriguing details might become a best-seller and lead to a blockbuster movie – and help Gilbert recover his company's rightful dues in a novel manner. And this paved the way toward the publication of CORPORATE DECEPTION.

When the manuscript of CORPORATE DECEPTION was completed, an offer to review its contents and raise objections on inaccuracies for amendments to be done was given to *Signode* and *Messrs David Lim & Partners* (Appendix 44) on 12 Jan 2011. The staff at *Signode* accepted the letter and acknowledged receipt. **The staff at Messrs David Lim & Partners also accepted the letter but after reading its contents refused to acknowledge receipt.** When *Gilbert* (who delivered the letter) requested for an acknowledgement, the staff consulted someone in the office and then informed him that **she was not going to accept the said letter and would deny having read it.** She then requested *Gilbert* to leave the premises, failing which she would call the "Security". *Gilbert* subsequently placed the said letter in the office and left the premises.

A book distributor informed *Gilbert* that for CORPORATE DECEPTION to be marketable, it was important to include accolades from individuals/institutions on the back cover; this was done through the distribution of advance reading copies to them before the final print run.

As *Messrs David Lim & Partners* had previously threatened to sue *Gilbert* for defamation (Appendix 39.2) and had even said that they would deny even having read his offer in a letter which he attempted to deliver to personally, he was advised that prior to distributing the advanced reading copies, notice be given to *Messrs David Lim & Partners*, *Signode* and *ITW Inc* through a law firm.

In early December 2011, *Gilbert* gave instructions to a law firm to give notice to *Messrs David Lim & Partners* together with an advance reading copy of CORPORATE DECEPTION, with an offer to them, *Signode* and *ITW Inc*, to review its contents for inaccuracies for the purpose of making necessary amendments accordingly.

Messrs David Lim & Partners failed/refused and/or neglected to accept the said offer and claimed that they were not retained by *Signode* and *ITW Inc* in respect of the matter and suggested that documents be forwarded directly to them. They further claimed that the lawyers in conduct of the legal action taken out by *Absolute* against *Signode* and *ITW Inc* (Chapter 15, pg 25) were no longer members of their firm and suggested that documents be forwarded directly to them.

Gilbert responded through his lawyers that *Signode* and *ITW Inc* had sought *Messrs David Lim & Partners'* representation in the matter involving the salient issues raised in the upcoming publication and hence had a duty to inform them of the offer to review the contents of the advance reading copy of CORPORATE DECEPTION. Furthermore, during the material time of the issues raised in the book and deliberated between all parties concerned, *Messrs David Lim & Partners* were not a limited liability partnership. *Messrs David Lim & Partners* refused to depart from their earlier position and with this impasse, *Gilbert* had no choice but to proceed with his endeavor to produce a marketable book without any further reference to *Messrs David Lim & Partners* – who had the interest of *Signode* and *ITW Inc* but chose not to do anything about it, for reasons best known to them.

Personal lives, family relationships and businesses are continually being ruined by unscrupulous lawyers, especially of high-heeled clients, through their God-given talents at the expense of justice for monetary gain and/or fame. The revelation in CORPORATE DECEPTION highlights only one such case. How many more have suffered a similar fate as *Absolute*? Perhaps lawyers who had attributed to dishonourable victories for their clients can answer this question.

Litigation is the basic legal right which guarantees every corporation its decade in Court.

David Porter

APPENDICES

APPENDIX 1

Cyklop – Signode joint venture in South East Asia.......

A Failure!

1. The managements and staffs of Cyklop and most of long service key staff (Admin, Marketing, Customer Service and Technical) has already set up their new business in Singapore.

2. With many years of experience in the market, the group of Cyklop key staffs already built up strong foundation for the future new business based on

3. Strong and outstanding relationship with key customers.

4. Strong personal relationship with the existing staff and strong team spirit which has been built for many years.

5. Super connection and trust with non- Cyklop or competition machines and material suppliers.

Great uncertainties of the joint venture of Cyklop and Signode

7. Good opportunity for convincing non- Cyklop competition supplier, customer, staff.

8. Some key staffs in Cyklop will remain in the joint venture company of CS Packaging and other staff of Cyklop will volunteer to be retrenched with retrenchment compensation. (this fund is then used as part of the setting up costs for this new company). Their work is to start up of the new company and tranfer all key Cyklop customers to the new company.

9. The key staffs of Cyklop will remain in control position in CS Packaging to
   1) Ensure all key existing Cyklop customers be able to transfer to the new company.
   2) Forward all important new sales leads, inquiries, tenders to the new company.
   3) Make sure the new company get important projects without competition or hard competition with Cyklop Signode- CS Packaging.
   4) Gather valuable Signode customers' information for the new company and eventually transfer these customers to the own new company.
   5) For consistent and high income under CS Packaging's operating expenses and at the same time, save on operating expenses during the initial start up for the new company.

10. Ensure immediate profit and risk free set up of new business.

11. The new company has already took some big projects.

The joint venture business of Cyklop and Signode in South East Asia will serve no purpose because of the above. There will be greater competition with this new company that have all old Cyklop team, Cyklop's key customers (and some Signode customers) and strong support with current strong "suppliers".

APPENDIX 2

ABSOLUTE TEC & SERVICES PTE LTD
221 HENDERSON ROAD #07-14 HENDERSON BUILDING SINGAPORE 159557
TEL: 274 5932, 274 5623, 339 3888, 339 6017 FAX: 276 0964, 339 7601
E-mail: taonb@mbox3.singnet.com.sg

ATS/PI/721

2 Mar 98

Ang Tan & Chang
200 Cantonment Road
#02-08 Southpoint
Singapore 089763

Attention: Ms Juliet Ang

Dear Ms Ang

INVESTIGATION SERVICES - STAFF CONDUCT

We would like to confirm that your client has accepted the following investigation package:

INVESTIGATION PACKAGE

Scope of work:

a.　Surveillance on the movement of one person for a period not exceeding 21 days.
b.　Supply and installation of telephone recording device at office premises for a period not exceeding 21 days:
c.　Carrying out supplementary investigation work to achieve company's objective.

Fee:　　　　$18,000/-
Contigency Fee: $12,000/- (payable only upon achleveing objective)

As we have already commenced work, we would appreciate if you could advise your client to forward us our retainer fee of $10,000.

Yours faithfully

APPENDIX 3

THE STRAITS TIMES : Thursday, April 2, 1998

INFORMATION SOUGHT

'INFORMATION IS SOUGHT on directors, employees or agents of CS PACKAGING CORPORATION (SINGAPORE) PTE LTD (formerly known as CYKLOP SINGAPORE PTE LTD and GERRARD-SIGNODE PTE LTD) who:

1. are in any way involved in or connected with a company or organisation whose business is similar to or in competition with CS PACKAGING CORPORATION (SINGAPORE) PTE LTD's business of industrial packaging, lifting and fastenings; and/or
2. might have acted in a manner detrimental to the interests of CS PACKAGING CORPORATION (SINGAPORE) PTE LTD.

A REWARD is offered for information leading to successful prosecution.

CS PACKAGING CORPORATION (SINGAPORE) PTE LTD will not hesitate to initiate civil and/or criminal proceedings against any party wilfully receiving, disseminating and/or using CS PACKAGING CORPORATION (SINGAPORE) PTE LTD's confidential information for gain or otherwise.

Please communicate with:
ANG TAN & CHANG
200 Cantonment Road #02-08
Southpoint, Singapore 089763
Tel: 221-0102, Fax: 227-6556, Email: atnc@pacific.net.sg

APPENDIX 4

CS PACKAGING CORPORATION (SINGAPORE) PTE LTD

INTERNAL INVESTIGATION

15TH APRIL 1998

PANEL: JULIET ANG (solicitor for CS Packaging Corporation (Singapore) Pte Ltd)

WILLIAM YAU (Executive Director & General Manager, CS Packaging Corporation (Hong Kong) Limited)

REPORT

1. The following persons were interviewed by the Panel:

2. The following persons did not show up for the interview:

4. Having heard the interviewees, the inescapable conclusion is that the actions of the Managing Director are irregular and not consistent with those expected of the chief executive officer of a company in that:
   • immediately after and since he tendered his resignation, he has been openly telling staff that he will be in business in competition with CSPC
   • he has ordered CSPC staff to make adjustments to customers' machines in order to accommodate strapping sold by competitors;
   • he appears to have diverted business away from CSPC to competitors;
   • he has concluded deals on very questionable terms.

APPENDIX 5

NO.	PART NO.	DESCRIPTION		ETA	ORD
1	Blue Tempered and Waxed Coated Steel Strapping				40tons
	Size	16mm x 0.50mm			
	Tensile Strength	Min. 75kg / mm²			
	Approx Weight	600 - 700kgs / coil			
	Elongation	2% - 4%			
	Hardness	90 - 100 HRB			
	Packing	15 rolls / pallet			
2	Blue Tempered and Waxed Coated Steel Strapping				23tons
	Size	19mm x 0.6mm			
	Tensile Strength	Min. 75kg / mm²			
	Approx Weight	700 - 800kgs / coil			
	Elongation	2% - 4%			
	Hardness	90 - 100 HRB			
	Packing	15 rolls / pallet			
	Blue Tempered and Waxed Coated Steel Strapping				40tons
	Size	32mm x 0.8mm			
	Tensile Strength	Min 75kg / mm²			
	Approx Weight	500 - 550kgs / coil			
	Elongation	2% - 4%			
	Hardness	90 - 100HRB			
	Packing	12 rolls / pallet			

APPENDIX 6

OMNIX INTERNATIONAL PTE LTD
221 Henderson Road, #07-14 Henderson Building, Singapore 154557
Tel: 274 5932 , 274 5683   Fax: 2760964

FAX TRANSMISSION

Date: 17 Jul 98

To: Hankook Metal Ind Co Ltd

Fax: 051 555 5088

Dear Sir

STEEL STRAPPING

Kindly give us your best offer for the following:

1.   Blue Tempered and Waxed Coated Steel Strapping
        Specifications
        Size   16mm x 0.50mm
        Tensile Strength   Min. 75kg/mm2
        Approx Weight   600 - 700 kgs / coil
        Elongation   2% - 4%
        Hardness   90 - 100 HRB
        Packing   15 rolls / pallet

        Quantity
        200 mt

2.   Blue Tempered and Waxed Coated Steel Strapping
        Specifications
        Size   19mm x 0.6mm
        Tensile Strength   Min. 75kg/mm2
        Approx Weight   700 - 800 kgs / coil
        Elongation   2% - 4%
        Hardness   90 - 100 HRB
        Packing   15 rolls / pallet

        Quantity
        200 mt

Best Regards

Ng Yong Huat

APPENDIX 6.1

OMNIX INTERNATIONAL PTE LTD
221 Henderson Road, #07-14 Henderson Building, Singapore 154557
Tel: 274 6932 , 274 6883   Fax: 2760984

FAX TRANSMISSION

Date: 27 Aug 98

To: SUMIPUTEH STEEL CENTRE SDN BHD

Fax: 0203 550 4033

Attn: Mr Lai
           Sales Department

Dear Mr Lai

STEEL STRAPPING

Further to our teleconversation this morning, kindly offer us your best price (FOB Port Klang) for blue tempered and waxed coated steel strapping of the following specifications & quantities:

Size	Hardness	Elongation	Packing	Quantity
19mm x 0.5 mm	90 - 100 HRB	2% - 4%	15 rolls/pallet	200 mt
19 mm x 0.6 mm	90 - 100 HRB	2% - 4%	15 rolls/pallet	200 mt

Best Regards

Gilbert Pereira
Director

58

APPENDIX 6.2

OMNIX INTERNATIONAL PTE LTD
221 Henderson Road, #07-14 Henderson Building, Singapore 154557
Tel: 274 5932 , 274 5683   Fax: 2760994

FAX TRANSMISSION

Date: 1 Sep 98

To: PACIFIC METAL INDUSTRY (SDN) BHD

Fax: 0203 368 0963

Attn: Mr Choo Teck Hock

Dear Mr Choo

STEEL STRAPPING

We obtained particulars of your company from MATRADE (Malayan Trade Board) in Singapore.

Further to our teleconversation this morning, kindly offer us your best price (FOB Port Klang) for blue tempered and waxed coated steel strapping of the following specifications & quantities:

Size	Hardness	Elongation	Packing	Quantity
19mm x 0.5 mm	90 - 100 HRB	2% - 4%	15 rolls/pallet	200 mt
19 mm x 0.6 mm	90 - 100 HRB	2% - 4%	15 rolls/pallet	200 mt

As we are a buying house, the price offered must be attractive. If you can meet up with our requirements, we can look towards a long term business relationship.

Best Regards

Gilbert Pereira
Director

APPENDIX 7

PACIFIC METAL INDUSTRY SDN. BHD.

No. 9, Leboh Raya Petal,
Pandamaran Industrial Area,
42000 Port Klang,
Selangor Darul Ehsan, Malaysia.
Tel: 03-3687304 (6 Lines)
Telefax: 03-3680963

3rd September 1998   Ref : cth.OI

To   : Connix International Pte Ltd   Fax : 2760964
Attn : Mr. Gilbert Pereira

From : Mr Choo Teck Hock

Dear Sir

RE : QUOTATION FOR STEEL STRAPPING.

We would like to quote you the following item your kind consideration.

A) Steel Strapping.
Brand   : Elephant (Japan Spec)
Quality   : Blue Tempered, Wax Coated and Smooth Finished.
i) Size   : 19mm x 0.5mm
  Hardness : 90 - 100 HRB
  Elongation : 2% - 4%
  Packing   : 15rolls/in bundle without pallet
  Quantity : 200mt
  Price   : RM1.85/kg

ii) Size   : 19mm x 0.6mm
  Hardness : 90 - 100 HRB
  Elongation : 2% - 4%
  Packing   : 15rolls/in bundle without pallet
  Quantity : 200mt
  Price   : RM1.85/kg

Term   : 30% prepayment/deposit required. Balance by irrevocable and confirmed
              L/C.
Validity   : Until 10th September 1998.
Delivery   : 2-4 weeks, after receipt of all required payments L/C subject to prior sales.

We sincerely hope our quotation is favourable to you and if you need further information
please do not hesitate to call us.

Thanks & regards.

APPENDIX 7.1

SUMIPUTEH STEEL CENTRE SDN.BHD (COMPANY NO 32083-U)
FAX :03-5506117 / 5504033   PAGE : 1/1

TO : OMNIX INTERNATIONAL PTE.LTD. ATTN : MR. *GILBERT PEREIRA* *< DIRECTOR >* FAX : *03 - 2760264.*	OUR REF :YGKSP 8891 DATE : 26/3/98 FROM : LAI

SUB : PRICE QUOTATION

WE ARE PLEASED TO QUOTE AS FOLLOWS :----

BLUE TEMPERED BALING HOOP(WAXED)

SIZE/MM   PRICE /MT
0.50 X 19 X C   RM 1880 /MT
0.35 X 19 X C   RM 1870 /MT

QTY :200 MT /SIZE

PRICE VALIDITY :TILL END OF SEPT'98 DELIVERY.

PAYMENT :CASH BEFORE DELIVERY.

DELIVERY PLACE :YOUR FORWARDER'S WAREHOUSE IN P/KLANG.

PACKING :EXPORT PACKING WITH STEEL ENVELOP.

DELIVERY LEAD TIME :ONE MONTH UPON ORDER CONFIRMATION.

WE ARE AWAITING YOUR EARLY REPLY, THANK YOU

REGARDS,

SUMIPUTEH STEEL CENTRE SDN. BHD,

Lui Gin Nian
Asst. Sales Manager

APPENDIX 7.2

HANKOOK METAL IND. CO., LTD.
HANKUM CO., LTD.
(421-3, Oncheon 2-Dong, Dong Rae-Gu, Busan, Korea)

FAX TRANSMISSION

TO : OMNEX INTERNATIONAL PTE LTD
ATTN: MR. NG YONG HUAT
FROM: B. C. KANG/J. K. KIM

DATE: JUL. 20, 1998
CITY : BUSAN, KOREA
NUMBER OF PAGES: 1/ 1
REF. NO. : 98-720C K

DEAR SIR,

THANK YOU FOR YOUR INQUIRY 17TH, JULY,

WE WOULD LIKE TO KNOW THE FOLLOWING QUESTION IN ORDER
TO QUOTE GOOD PRICE FOR YOU.
1) HOW DO YOU KNOW OUR COMPANY ?
2) WHERE DO YOU GET STEEL STRAPPING NOW ?
3) WHAT IS THE CONSUMPTION PER MONTH ?
4) WHERE IS YOUR SALES TERRITORY ?
5) PLEASE EXPLAIN THIS "APPROX WEIGHT : 600-700KGS/COIL &
   700-800 KGS/COIL" AGAINST COIL WEIGHT OR PALLET WEIGHT ?

YOUR KIND COOPERATION WOULD BE HIGHLY APPRECIATED.

THANK YOU,
BEST REGARDS,
J. K. KIM

TEL. : 82-51-555-4051 (REP.)
FAX. : 82-51-555-5088

APPENDIX 8

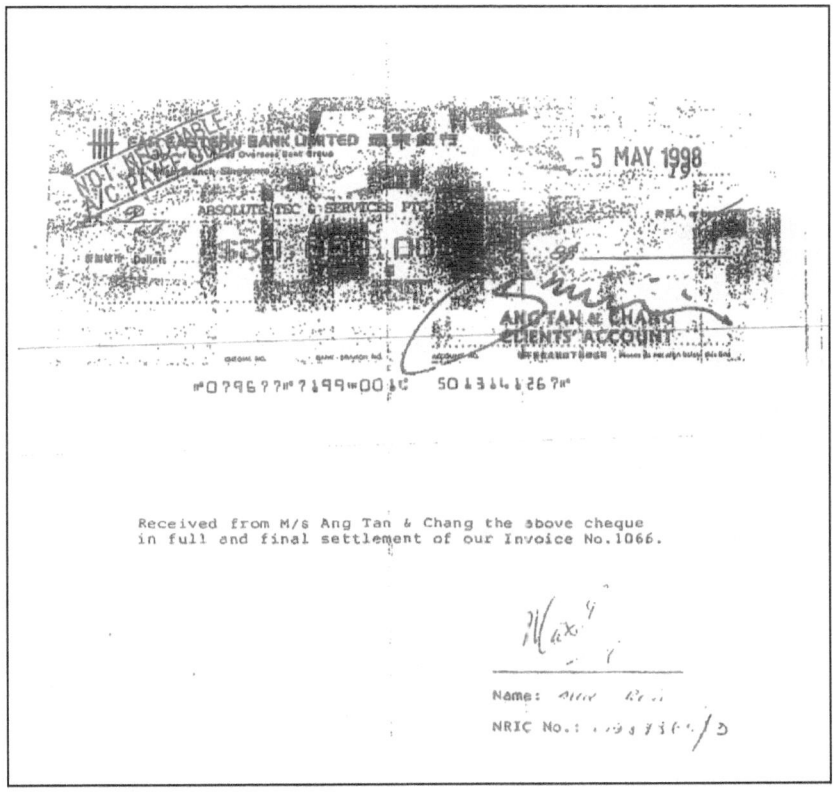

Received from M/s Ang Tan & Chang the above cheque
in full and final settlement of our Invoice No.1066.

Name: _____

NRIC No.: _____

APPENDIX 9

IN THE SUBORDINATE COURTS OF THE REPUBLIC OF SINGAPORE

D C Suit No.　　　)
6013 of 1998　　　)

Between

ABSOLUTE TEC & SERVICES PTE LTD
(RC No. 198803366C)

... *Plaintiffs*

And

CS PACKAGING CORPORATION PTE LTD
(RC No. 199700197D)

... *Defendants*

SUMMONS FOR FURTHER DIRECTIONS

LET ALL PARTIES concerned attend before the Judge/Registrar in Chambers on the　　　day of 1 7 JUN 1999 1999, at　　030　　a.m./p.m. in the Subordinate Courts, 1 Havelock Square, Singapore 059724 on the hearing of an application on the part of the Plaintiffs for the following orders that:-

1. the Defendants do produce to this Court the following document namely, an anonymous letter received by the Defendants from Malaysia, after the advertisement exhibited at page 30 of Anthony Tseng Chia Kang's affidavit, appeared in The Straits Times on 2 April 1998.

2. costs of and occasioned by this application be to the Plaintiffs in any event.

The grounds of this application are set out in the Affidavit of Gilbert Pereira filed herein.

Dated this　　day of 1 5 JUN 1999　1999

Entered No. 311780 of 1999

Clerk　　 Qy

Foo Chee Hock
Senior Deputy Registrar
DEPUTY REGISTRAR

APPENDIX 10

April 4, 1998

Ang Tan & Chang
200 Cantonment Road,
#02-08 Southpoint, Singapore 089763.

Re: Your Notice In The Straits Times dated April 2,1998

I had read your notice in S.T. on April 2, 1998 with great interest.

I act as an individual who has long business dealing with these companies mentioned and is writing in for two main reasons, i.e. for the benefits and good future of CS Packaging, and to be rewarded as stated.

Preliminarily, I can offer solid evidents for below:

- Improper business conduct and practice from 1992 for both Malaysia and Singapore.
- "Contraband" items re-sold in early nineties,
- Conflicting businesses presently running by few key managers of Malaysia and Singapore.
- Information leakage to some American, German, Italian and Swiss competitors
- Siphoning on share-holders funds through connected suppliers and vendors.

Before my actual contact with you, you must perceive what will happen if above are brought to the court of law because this involves few top level people "present and past".

You must also guarantee full anonymous status to protect my identity.

Myself will give you one week to think of the above and probable bigger reward amount for your discussion with your clients.

I will call you by April 11, 1998 using password "KTBW" before talking.

Best regards

KTBW

APPENDIX 11

Writer's e-mail : cmchang@trc.com.sg
Writer's DID : 6539 1682

OUR REF: CM/ct/1999/926A
YOUR REF:

Tan Rajah & Cheah

5 December 2002

Straits Trading Building
9 Battery Road #15-00
Singapore 049910

Messrs Signode Singapore Pte Ltd
(formerly known as CS Packaging Corporation (S) Pte Ltd
2 Joo Koon Circle, Jurong
Singapore 629031   Attn: Mr Toh Boon Leng
                                     General Manager

Telephone 6532 2271
Fax   6535 2475 (General)
         6532 2633 (Litigation)
         6536 2275 (Conveyancing)
E-Mail: trc@trc.com.sg

Service of court documents
by facsimile is not accepted.

Dear Sirs

District Court Appeal No. 23 of 1999
DC Suit No. 6013 of 1998
Amicable Settlement on Outstanding Professional Investigation Fees

We act for Messrs Absolute Tec & Services Pte Ltd of 38A Jalan
Pemimpin, #02-04 Wisdom Building, Singapore 577179.

We are instructed that by an agreement entered into vide your company,
you engaged the professional services of our clients to procure evidence
on your former managing director. After our clients had completed their
assignment, your former managing director was released from his
employment conditionally; one of which was that he had to forego his
gratuity – which was the objective of our clients' assignment (you may
wish to inspect the documents pertaining to this at our office).

Our clients were paid their professional fees in partial for the assignment
undertaken. Their attempt to recover their balance fees became futile
when your company denied the salient terms of the agreement on their
appointment. Our clients' resort to seek redress through the courts was
thwarted by a defective action that was filed against you on 14 Oct 1998.
Our clients addressed this issue in Court by way of a writ against their
previous solicitors for professional negligence. A settlement was reached
wherein our clients were partially compensated for the legal costs incurred
in this respect. As the Court did not bar them from taking out a fresh
action against you, our clients did not pursue the fresh action yet but have
reserved their rights to do so.

In the meantime, our clients understand that you had engaged the services
of an international risk consulting company, namely Kroll Associates (S)
Pte Ltd, to advise you on the matter. We are instructed that our clients
had handed over various documents to Kroll and had given their full
cooperation in order for them to advise you on the matter. However, till
to date, nothing has evolved up to this stage and our clients are
disappointed.

L T Lim
C R Rajah (Senior Counsel)
C S Tan
S H Almenoar
Y K Cheong
C Mohan
L S Lim
K F Han
Khoo Ghee Saik
Imran H Khwaja
A Kurthigesu
W J M Ricquier
David Khor
Caroline Ho
Sravana Barasham
Zahara Bakar
Sugidha Nithi
Burton N C Chen
K J Chew
Rudy Gunaratnam

Assistants
Lucy Khoo Bee Lay
Khaleel Namazie
Kathleen S. Gomez
Vaani Rajah
Reji Ramason
Michelle Jeganathan
M K Eusuff Ali
Archana Patel
Tricia Feng
Dave J S Panneeh
Moiz H Sibhawalla
Adrian T J Tan
Clarissa S L Yong
Lalitha Rajah
Christine P S Lee

Advocates & Solicitors
Notaries Public
Commissioners for Oaths
Agents for Trademarks

APPENDIX 11.1

DATE: 5 December 2002

TO: Messrs Signode Singapore Pte Ltd

— 2 —

Please note that our clients had incurred financial losses through legal costs and bank interest charges which amount to over $137,000; of which only $67,000 was recovered through the settlement mentioned above. Our clients also suffered non-tangible damages, ranging from partnership discord, mistrust amongst operatives, stress, cancellation of various assignments, etc. during their original claim against you.

We have been instructed that your leading witness suppressed crucial evidence during the original claim against your company. Our clients have since procured evidence to support their case that your leading witness was dishonest and therefore would seek to impeach his evidence should our clients decide to pursue a fresh action against your company. However, with the view to resolving this matter amicably and expeditiously, our clients are prepared to work out an amicable settlement with you.

Please let us have your reply as soon as possible.

Yours faithfully

Tan Rajah & Cheah

for Chandra Mohan K Nair
Tan Rajah & Cheah

cc   client

Messrs Absolute Tec & Services Pte Ltd
38A Jalan Pemimpin
#02-04 Wisdom Building
Singapore 577179

By Fax only : 6259 4232
Attn: Mr Gilbert Pereira

APPENDIX 12

---

tecnix

From:	"andrew beeson" <abeeson@compuserve.com>
To:	"tecnix" <tecnix@singnet.com.sg>
Cc:	"Toh Boon Leng" <marctoh@singnet.com.sg>
Sent:	Monday, April 07, 2003 1:47 PM
Subject:	OUTSTANDING FEES

Gilbert

I have passed a copy of the letter from your Lawyers to our Lawyers in Singapore. I have also passed a copy to our Head Office Legal Counsel in Chicago.
I will also provide them with previous correspondence which I have at hand.

You previously dealt with our Advisers - Kroll in Singapore. Kroll have since closed their office in Singapore and moved their people offshore.

I am not able to negotiate directly with you on this issue, therefore I advise you to wait until our Lawyers are in contact with you or your Lawyers..

Regards

ANDREW

APPENDIX 13

DAVID LIM & PARTNERS

advocates & solicitors • commissioners for oaths
notaries public • trademark agents

Your Ref   : CM/ct/1999/926A
Our Ref   : JC/LP/2001-00041-6/sl

24 April 2003

M/S TAN RAJAH & CHEAH
9 Battery Road #15-00
Straits Trading Building
Singapore 049910

BY FAX & POST
(fax no. 6532 2633)

Attention: Mr Chandra Mohan K Nair

Dear Sirs

AMICABLE SETTLEMENT ON OUTSTANDING PROFESSIONAL INVESTIGATION FEES

We act for M/s Signode Singapore Pte Ltd

We refer to your letter dated 5 December 2002 (addressed to our clients) which has been handed to us.

We write to inform you that we are in the process of taking our clients' instructions and would appreciate if you would kindly hold your hands on the matter in the meantime.

All our clients' rights are strictly reserved.

Your faithfully

DAVID LIM & PARTNERS

consultant
TANG SEE CHIN
partners
DAVID T.L. LIM
YVONNE TAN
SURESH DAMODARA
AW EE TUAN
LEONARD HAZRA
KESAVAN NAIR
CHEONG CHUH FENG
JONATHAN FOONG
K SURESHAN
solicitors
SUNIL S. GILL
DIANA THE HUI LING
LONG JEK AUN
CHAN HOE
SAMUEL YUEN
WINSTON WONG

RECEIVED
24 APR 2003
TAN RAJAH
& CHEAH

APPENDIX 14

DAVID LIM
& PARTNERS

advocates & solicitors • commissioners for oaths
notaries public • trademark agents

your ref	:	
our ref	:	AET/AW/97-81-4/ie
via fax	:	6532 2633
via email	:	
no. of pages	:	
(inclusive of this page)		
writer's did	:	6531 0238
writer's email address	:	angelinewong@dlplaw.com.sg

18 March 05

Messrs Tan Rajah & Cheah
Singapore

Attention: Mr Chandra Mohan K Nair

Dear Sirs

AMICABLE SETTLEMENT ON OUTSTANDING PROFESSIONAL INVESTIGATION FEES

We refer to your fax of 17 March 2005.

We will be seeking our clients' instruction. However, as our clients are based in the United States, more time would be required for communications between us. Our clients would also require time to decide on your proposal.

As such, we may not be able to revert by 21 March 2005. We will nonetheless try to revert as soon as possible, some time next week.

Yours faithfully

David Lim & Partners
Angeline Wong

cc   clients

H:\Corporate\Corp_Shared\Angeline\JTW - Hydra\TRC.F6.doc

consultant
TANG SEE CHIM
partners
DAVID T.L. LIM
YVONNE TAN
SURESH DAMODARA
AW EE TUAN
LEONARD HAZRA
KESAVAN NAIR
CHEONG CHUH FENG
JONATHAN FOONG
K SURESHAN
SUNIL S. GILL
JOANNA TENG
DIANA THE HUI LING

RECEIVED
18 MAR 2005
TAN RAJAH
& CHEAH

APPENDIX 15

DAVID LIM
& PARTNERS

advocates & solicitors • commissioners for oaths
notaries public • trade mark agents

your ref	:	CM/sl/1999/926A
our ref	:	AET/AW/97-81-4/ie
via fax	:	6532 2633
via email	:	
no. of pages	:	
(inclusive of this page)		
writer's did	:	6531 0238
writer's email address	:	angelinewong@dlplaw.com.sg

14 April 05

Messrs Tan Rajah & Cheah
Singapore

Attention: Mr Chandra Mohan K Nair

Dear Sirs

AMICABLE SETTLEMENT ON OUTSTANDING PROFESSIONAL INVESTIGATION FEES

We refer to your fax of 4 April 2005.

We have been instructed by our clients that they would not be attending the proposed meeting. Nonetheless, our clients are open to your clients setting out any proposal which your clients may have in writing for the consideration of our clients.

Yours faithfully

David Lim & Partners
Angeline Wong

cc clients

H:\Corporate\Corp_Shared\Angeline\JTW - Hydra\TRC.F7.doc

consultant
TANG SEE CHIM

partners
DAVID T.L. LIM
YVONNE TAN
SURESH DAMODARA
AW EE TUAN
LEONARD HAZRA
KESAVAN NAIR
CHEONG CHUH FENG
JONATHAN FOONG
K SURESHAN
SUNIL S. GILL
JOANNA TENG
DIANA THE HUI LING

RECEIVED
14 APR 2005
TAN RAJAH
& CHEAH

APPENDIX 16

OUR REF: CM/si/1999/926A
YOUR REF: AET/AW/97-81-4/ie

trc
Tan Rajah & Cheah

21 April 2005   By Fax & Post : 6532 0122

M/s David Lim & Partners
50 Raffles Place #17-01
Singapore Land Tower
Singapore 048623

Straits Trading Building
9 Battery Road #15-00
Singapore 049910

Telephone 6532 2271
Facsimile 6535 2475 (General)
          6532 2633 (Litigation)
          6536 2275 (Conveyancing)
E-Mail   trc@trc.com.sg
Website   www.trc.com.sg

Service of court documents
by facsimile is not accepted.

Attention : Ms Angeline Wong

Dear Sirs,

Re: Amicable Settlement on Outstanding Professional Investigation
      fees

We refer to your letter of 14 Apr 2005.

Our clients convey their gratitude to your clients on their willingness to consider their proposal for an amicable settlement of this matter.

Our clients have incurred losses amounting to about $350,000.00 in the matter by way of their outstanding professional fees ($152,000.00), legal costs ($106,000.00) and interest incurred ($86,000.00) during this trying period. Our clients would appreciate if your clients could settle this matter by your clients paying to our clients the equivalent of the said outstanding professional fees of $152,000.00 as full and final settlement in this matter.

We look forward to your clients' prompt acceptance of our clients' offer of an amicable settlement.

Yours faithfully

Chandra Mohan K Nair
Tan Rajah & Cheah

cc   client   By Fax & Post : 6259 4232

Messrs Absolute Tec & Services Pte Ltd
38A Jalan Pemimpin
#02-04 Wisdom Building
Singapore 577179   Attn : Mr Gilbert Pereira

L T Lim
C R Rajah (Senior Counsel)
C S Tan
Y K Cheong
C Mohan
K F Han
Khoo Ghee Saik
Imran H Khwaja
A Karthigesu
Sayana Baratham
Zahara Bakar
Sugidha Nithi
Burton N C Chen
K J Chew

Consultants
Caroline Ho
Lucy Khoo Bee Lay
Y K Cheong
Assistants
Vaani Rajah
Raji Ramason
Michelle Jeganathan
M K Eusuff Ali
Archana Patel
Moiz H Sithawalla
Chen Chee Yen
Adrian T J Tan
Lalitha Rajah
Cheryl S T Lim
Brenton C K Chen
Lee Terk Yang
Owyong Eu Gene
Lavinia Rajah

APPENDIX 17

OUR REF CM/si/1999/926A
YOUR REF RA.CIV1230.2005.as

Tan Rajah ...

9 June 2005   By Fax Only : 6438 0220

Straits Trading Building
9 Battery Road #13-00
Singapore 049910

M/s Riaz, Ian Chang & Pat Quah
133 New Bridge Road #15-09
Chinatown Point
Singapore 059413

Telephone 6532 2271
Facsimile   6535 2475 (General)
           6532 2633 (Litigation)
           6536 2275 (Conveyance)
E-Mail   trc@trc.com.sg
Website   www.trc.com.sg

Service of court documents
by facsimile is not accepted.

Dear Sirs

Re: Amicable Settlement on Outstanding Professional
       Investigation fees

We refer to your letter to us dated 8 June 2005.

We have no objections.

Yours faithfully

Chandra Mohan K Nair
Tan Rajah & Cheah

Cc   client

M/s Absolute Tec & Services Pte Ltd
Attention : Mr Gilbert Pereira
By Fax only : 6259 4232

L T Lim
C R Rajah (Senior Couns
C S Tan
Y K Cheong
C Mohan
K F Han
Khoo Ghee Saik
Imran H Khwaja
A Karthigesu
Suyana Baratham
Zahara Bakar
Sugidha Nithu
Burton N C Chen
K J Chew

Consultants
Caroline Ho
Lucy Khoo Bee Lay
Y K Cheong
Assistants
Vaani Rajah
Raji Ramason
Michelle Jaganathan
M K Eusuff Ali
Archana Patel
Moiz H Sithawalla
Chen Chee Yen
Adrian T J Tan
Lalitha Rajah
Cheryl S P Lim
Brenton C X Chen
Lee Terk Yang
 Owyong Lu Gene
Lavinia Rajah

APPENDIX 18

RIAZ, IAN CHANG & PAT QUAH
ADVOCATES AND SOLICITORS

Your Reference: AET/AW/97-81-4/le

Our Reference: *RA.CIV1230.2005.as*

PATRICIA QUAH (LLB HON
IAN CHANG   (LLB HON
RIAZ QAYYUM (LLB HON

14th June 2005

Messrs David Lim & Partners
50 Raffles Place #17-01
Singapore Land Tower
Singapore 048623

BY FAX ONLY
(Fax No. 65320122)
(Total: 1 Page)

Dear Sirs

RE: AMICABLE SETTLEMENT ON OUTSTANDING PROFESSIONAL INVESTIGATION FEES

We act for Messrs Absolute Tec & Services Pte Ltd and have taken over conduct of this matter from Messrs Tan Rajah & Cheah.

Our instructions are as follows:-

(1)   This matter has dragged on long enough.

(2)   Our clients have made every effort to be reasonable, apparently to no avail.

(3)   On an absolutely without prejudice basis, our clients, despite substantial loss to themselves, have offered to accept $152,000.00 being their outstanding fees only.

(4)   Our clients hope that your clients can confirm this without any further delay.

(5)   In the event that this matter has to proceed, our clients will claim the full amount due to them including aggravated damages.

(6)   Our clients also have information that may be potentially embarrassing to various parties.

(7)   Our clients are also exploring the possibility of taking action directly in the United States in view of fresh developments in the matter.

However, our clients, without prejudice to their full rights, and purely to resolve the matter amicably, can accept an amount of $152,000.00 in full and final settlement of this long outstanding matter. We trust your clients will be sensible about this matter.

Kindly revert **within 7 days**.

Yours faithfully

c.c.   clients

74

APPENDIX 19

IN THE SUBORDINATE COURTS OF THE REPUBLIC OF SINGAPORE

DC Suit No. 3693 of 2005/W

Between

ABSOLUTE TEC & SERVICES PTE LTD
(RC NO. 198803366C)

...Plaintiff

And

1. SIGNODE SINGAPORE PTE LTD
   (formerly known as CS Packaging
   Corporation (Singapore) Pte Ltd)
   (RC NO. 197700197D)
2. ILLINOIS TOOL WORKS INC.
   (ID No. not applicable)

...Defendants

AFFIDAVIT

I, TOH BOON LENG (NRIC No. S1640788G) care of No. 2 Joo Koon Circle, Jurong, Singapore 629031, do make oath and say as follows: -

1. I am a director of the 1st Defendant and I am duly authorised by the 1st Defendant to affirm this affidavit on its behalf.

2. The facts deposed to herein are within my personal knowledge, information and belief and insofar as they are not, they are obtained from documents/papers in my possession/power and are true to the best of my knowledge information and belief.

3. I make this affidavit in support of the 1st Defendant's application under Order 14 rule 12 of the Rules of Court for an Order that the Plaintiff's claim against the 1st

7. Mr Pereira is basically making up an allegation of an agreement in March 2002 (which does not exist) in order to support his claims against the Defendants. I am advised and believe that this amounts to an abuse of the process of the Court and should not be countenanced.

APPENDIX 20

IN THE SUBORDINATE COURTS OF THE REPUBLIC OF SINGAPORE

DC Suit No. 3693 of 2005/W

Between

ABSOLUTE TEC & SERVICES PTE LTD
(RC NO. 198803366C)

...Plaintiff

And

1. **SIGNODE SINGAPORE PTE LTD**
   (formerly known as CS Packaging
   Corporation (Singapore) Pte Ltd)
   (RC NO. 197700197D)
2. **ILLINOIS TOOL WORKS INC.**
   (ID No. not applicable)

...Defendants

DEFENCE OF THE 1ST DEFENDANT

9. Paragraph 20 of the Statement of Claim is admitted. The 1st Defendant appointed M/s Kroll Associates Pte Ltd ("Kroll") to investigate the Plaintiff's claim against the 1st Defendant as part of a due diligence exercise which was carried out when the new management of the 1st Defendant started managing the 1st Defendant's business affairs. Any work carried out by Kroll was work done in contemplation of legal proceedings and for the purposes of obtaining legal advice on the Plaintiff's claim and therefore privileged.

APPENDIX 21

IN THE SUBORDINATE COURTS OF THE REPUBLIC OF SINGAPORE

DC Suit No. 3693 of 2005/W

Between

ABSOLUTE TEC & SERVICES PTE LTD
(RC NO. 198803366C)

...Plaintiff

And

1. **SIGNODE SINGAPORE PTE LTD**
    (formerly known as CS Packaging
    Corporation (Singapore) Pte Ltd)
    (RC NO. 197700197D)
2. **ILLINOIS TOOL WORKS INC.**
    (ID No. not applicable)

...Defendants

SKELETAL SUBMISSIONS OF THE 1ST DEFENDANT

THE PLAINTIFF'S CASE

1. The Plaintiff commenced proceedings against the 1st Defendant in DC Suit No. 6013 of 1998 (filed on 14 October 1998), for the sum of S$152,000.00. The basis of the Plaintiff's claim were alleged agreements whereby the Plaintiff rendered investigation services in return for an alleged fixed contingent fee.

2. It therefore cannot be disputed that, at the time DC Suit No. 6013 of 1998 was commenced on 14 October 1998, the Plaintiff took the position that its alleged claim had already been crystallised and that whatever work it is alleged that it was supposed to carry out for the 1st Defendant had been concluded by then.

5e. The Plaintiff has concocted an alleged greement in paragraph 18 of the Statement of Claim to justify its right to commence fresh proceedings against the 1st Defendant.

13. The Plaintiff, in view of its difficulties as detailed above, has concocted a strategy whereby it asserts the existence of an alleged oral agreement between the Plaintiff and the Defendants in March 2002 (the "Alleged Oral Agreement").

APPENDIX 22

Essential Requirements of a Valid Compromise

INTRODUCTION

Since a compromise is merely a contract, the ordinary principles of 3–01 contract law apply with as much force as in other contractual contexts. Under the ordinary law a contract will not be found to have arisen unless:

    (i) consideration exists[1];
    (ii) an agreement can be identified which is complete and certain;
    (iii) the parties intend to create legal relations; and
    (iv) in some cases, certain formalities have been observed.[2]

The significance of each of these requirements in the context of compromise will be examined briefly.

CONSIDERATION

The usual approach to consideration under the general law is to define it as 3–02 the accrual of some benefit to one party or the suffering of some detriment by the other.[3] Consideration may consist of the exchange of mutual promises or the performance by one party of an act in return for a promise by the other to do some act.[4] In standard terminology, consideration must "move from the promisee".[5]

"Every day a compromise is effected on the grounds that the party 3–08 making it has a chance of succeeding in it, and if he bona fide believes he has a fair chance of success, he has a reasonable ground for suing, and his forbearance to sue will constitute a good consideration. When such a person forbears to sue he gives up what he believes to be a right of action, and the other party gets an advantage, and, instead of being annoyed with an action, he escapes from the vexations incident to it . . ."[14]

APPENDIX 23

1

A

18th May 2006

In Chambers

Before me

Sd: Terence Chua

B

Deputy Registrar

DC 3693 of 2005

SUM 272 of 2006 .

C

Between

ABSOLUTE TEC & SERVICES PTE LTD
(RC No. 198893366C)

... Plaintiff(s)

And

D

SIGNODE SINGAPORE PTE LTD
(RC No. 197700197D)

ILLINOIS TOOL WORKS INC
(ID No. not known)

... Defendant(s)

E

Coram: Deputy Registrar, Terence Chua

Mr Vijay [M/s Vijay & Company] – for Plaintiffs

Mr Sunil Singh [M/s David Lim & Partners] – for 1st Defendants

1D/C: (Written submissions)

APPENDIX 23.1

Notes of Evidence
DC 3693 of 2005
SUM 272 of 2006

A

P/C: Course of action arises from compromise, not original action. (Written submissions)

1D/C: Sea-Land Service: Court found that there was no forbearance to sue and therefore no basis for the contract.

B

Question is still whether or not Plaintiff had a case of action prior to compromise.

Forbearance to sue based on frivolous, vexatious or illegal claim with no consideration.

C

Frivolous or vexatious is in itself an abuse of process.

Miles v. New Zealand – if case is vexatious, it is independent of knowledge – they have no right to bring the case.

D

P/C: Res judicata has to be decided on the merits. Lawler v. Gray – principle in Henderson not "words of a statute" - doctrine to be applied where it is an abuse of process.

E

1D/C: Not in the public interest that should have multiplicity of proceedings. Decision in 1998 was on its merits despite what P/C says – decision on law is also decision on merits.

Court: The cause of action in this case is founded on the compromise agreement – however, the consideration is for a

APPENDIX 23.2

Notes of Evidence
DC 3693 of 2005
SUM 272 of 2006

A

forbearance to sue – which is to say, forbearance to sue on what? That links in all the way back to the 1998 Suit, which itself no longer exists, and to latch on to that as a course of action would both be res judicata in the extended sense and an abuse of process to get around the time bar. As a result,

B

the compromise of 2002 lacks the basis of that consideration to begin with and therefore could not be a valid contract.

I am therefore allowing the Defendant's application. The Plaintiff's claim is struck out.

C

Costs fixed at $5,000.

Sd: DR Terence Chua

CERTIFIED TRUE COPY

D

TERENCE CHUA
District Judge/Magistrate

E

APPENDIX 24

ABSOLUTE TEC & SERVICES PTE LTD
38A Jalan Pemimpin #02-04 Wisdom Building Singapore 577179
Tel: (65) 6259 2353 (65) 6259 5756 Fax: (65) 6259 4232
E-mail: tecnix@singnet.com.sg
Company Registration No: 19880336C

ATS/1048/06

7 Jun 2006

Commercial Affairs Department
391 New Bridge Road #06-701
Police Cantonment Complex, Block D
Singapore 088762

Attention: Director, CAD

Dear Sir

REQUEST FOR ASSISTANCE

1.   We are a private investigation agency that undertook an assignment for Signode (S) Pte Ltd (formerly known as CS Packaging Corporation Pte Ltd) sometime in March 1998. Signode briefed us that its former managing director (hereinafter referred to as Subject A) was suspected of being engaged in activities that were in breach of his fiduciary duties. We were required to procure evidence to confirm the said breaches as Signode wanted to penalize Subject A accordingly.

2.   Midway through our assignment, we received a response from an advertisement (Annex A) that was placed in the Straits Times. This response was a letter (Annex B) that implicated various key officers of Signode for serious business improprieties. However, we were instructed by Signode to regard the said letter as nonsensical and not to pursue our investigations on it. Shortly after, we were told to halt our investigations completely as Subject A, after being confronted with some of the evidence that we had procured, had offered to accept the following penalties in lieu of any legal action against him:

    a.   Forfeiture of his gratuity payment (about $250,000.00)
    b.   Reimbursement of legal costs incurred by Signode (about $56,000.00)
    c.   Undertaking not to directly or indirectly take part in any business similar or in competition with Signode.

3.   Signode promised us that as Subject A had been penalized, we would be entitled to the balance of our professional investigation fees amounting to $182,000.00. Subsequently, Signode paid our agency a sum of $30,000.00 and informed us that the final balance amount of $152,000.00 would be paid to us indirectly as our appointment in the matter was confidential and unknown to its top management.

...continued

APPENDIX 24.1

4.   When the balance amount was not forthcoming, we took out a writ of summons against Signode. Unfortunately, our action (DC Suit No. 6013 of 1998) was dismissed on a preliminary point of law due to defective pleadings. We took legal action against our lawyers for professional negligence and were reimbursed for all our legal costs incurred in pursuing the defective claim against Signode. However, we did not receive any compensation for our balance professional investigation fees of $152,000.00 as we were told that we could still take out a fresh action against Signode to claim the said amount.

5.   In the course of our preparations to commence a fresh action against Signode, we received a tip off that Signode's key witness (hereinafter referred to as Subject B) in DC Suit No. 6013 of 1998 had committed suicide whilst being investigated by the police for business improprieties that were highlighted in the letter referred to in para 2 above. Our attempts to confirm this hearsay evidence with the police were futile. Hence, we commenced our own investigations to establish the veracity of the said hearsay evidence.

6.   Our own investigations on the hearsay evidence established the following:

    a.   Subject B and the second witness in DC No. 6013 of 1998 (hereinafter referred to as Subject C) were investigated upon by an international investigation agency (www.krollworldwide.com) for serious business improprieties.

    b.   When the earlier mentioned investigation agency had completed its investigations on Subject B & C, Signode proceeded to take disciplinary action against them. Unfortunately, Subject B committed suicide when the CAD called him for an interview whilst Subject C was terminated.

7.   We have trying very hard to get legal redress on the injustice done to us by the false testimonies in DC Suit No. 6013 of 1998 but are facing an uphill task as a director of Signode is now affirming the evidence given in DC Suit No. 6013 of 1998 as being a true and fair account – when he is aware that Subject B had tendered in false evidence in the said suit and had committed serious business improprieties within the company. In so doing, we believe the said director had breached Section 157 of the Companies Act by not having acted honestly and using reasonable diligence in the discharge of the duties of his office. We have lost the first round because of the dishonesty of this director as he had managed to convince the Court that evidence in DC No. 5013 of 1998 was sound when in fact it has been tainted.

-2-

APPENDIX 24.2

8.   We are now preparing for the second round and our lawyer have told us that our allegations on the evidence in DC No. 6013 of 1998 being tainted cannot be admitted in Court because it is based on hearsay evidence. In this respect, we would be very grateful if you could assist us in the following, which we intend to raise:

        a.   to confirm hearsay evidence that Subject B was investigated upon by the CAD;

        b.   to confirm hearsay evidence that Subject B had committed suicide to avoid criminal prosecution when he was called upon for an interview by the CAD;

        c.   to confirm hearsay evidence that the investigations conducted by CAD on Subject B has a plausible link to the allegations on business improprieties stated in the letter referred to in paragraph 2 above.

9.   We would also appreciate any other assistance you could grant us in this matter to put right the travesty of justice that had befallen on us, as Signode is now using technical arguments to camouflage the criminal actions of Subject B. Our agency has suffered tremendously as a result of the false allegations contained in DC Suit No. 6013 of 1998. In the past, we have done assignments under the Official Secrets Act and have successfully concluded these cases with convictions where jail sentences and hefty fines were imposed on the subjects of our investigations. However, with the current state of affairs, we are unable to accept such assignments again because of the low morale as our credibility has been seriously affected.

Yours faithfully

Gilbert A. Pereira
Director

Enc.

APPENDIX 25

CAD.YAB.15208-M
ATS/0148/06

DID: 6557 5457
FAX: 6223 3171

19 June 2006

Mr Gilbert A Pereira
Director
M/s Absolute Tec & Services Pte Ltd
38A Jalan Pemimpin
#02-04 Wisdom Building
Singapore 577179

FAX: 6259 4232

Dear Sir

REQUEST FOR ASSISTANCE

We refer to your request dated 7 June 2006 to confirm your hearsay evidence concerning Subject B.

2. We regret to inform you that we are unable to assist you in the matter as the information arising from our police investigations is strictly confidential.

Yours faithfully

LIM KOK MENG
HEAD MARITIME & INVESTMENT FRAUD BRANCH
COMMERCIAL AFFAIRS DEPARTMENT
SINGAPORE POLICE FORCE

APPENDIX 26

IN THE SUBORDINATE COURTS OF THE REPUBLIC OF SINGAPORE

DC Suit No. 3693 of 2005/W

Between

ABSOLUTE TEC & SERVICES PTE LTD
(RC NO. 198803366C)

... Plaintiff

And

1. **SIGNODE SINGAPORE PTE LTD**
   (RC NO. 197700197D)
2. **ILLINOIS TOOL WORKS INC.**
   (RC NO. NOT APPLICABLE)

... Defendants

PLAINTIFF'S FURTHER
SKELETAL ARGUMENT

---

1.   The issue is whether the dismissal of the Plaintiff's action in DC Suit No. 6013 of 1998 by District Judge Wong Sheng Kwai on 23 June 1999 under the provision of O. 14 r 12 (see p. 83 & 84 of Plaintiff's affidavit dated 15 February 2006) is res judicata and estopped the Plaintiff from this action herein.

2.   At the outset we wish to humbly submit that O.14 r 12 gives the Court a wide discretion to dismiss the matter only if it can be completely

APPENDIX 26.1

2

disposed off on a point of law or on a matter of construction of a document.

3. However a dismissal under O.14 r 12 may not necessarily estoppe the Plaintiff from recommencing the same action again. For example, in a landlord and tenant situation, if the landlord action to evict a tenant is dismissed on the basis that the notice to quit is bad under the provision of O. 14 r 12 the landlord can always reissue another notice to quit and bring a fresh action against the tenant.

4. When an action or application is dismissed after a hearing, it is necessary to determine what matters beyond the actual dismissal concludes the parties. This depends on whether the dismissal involved the determination of any particular issue of fact or law, otherwise it only decides that the party has been refused relief.

See para 56, pg. 29 of doctrine of res judicata annexed herein (Annex 1).

For examples of cases where the Court has dismissed an action after hearing has commenced but they do not amount to an estoppel are set out also in the same para 56, pg. 29 & 30 of the Annex 1 herein.

APPENDIX 26.2

3

5.   Where a proceeding has been dismissed, no finding of fact will establish estoppel unless it was necessary to the dismissal.

However on the other hand, the dismissal of an application, which is not pursued will clearly give rise to an issue of estoppel. See para 56, pg 31 of the same annexure.

6.   In the earlier case DC Suit No. 6013 of 1998 although the action was dismissed under O.14 rule 12 on the basis that the claim was against public policy, no determination was made on the amount owing by the defendants to the Plaintiff.

7.   The Plaintiff is now not pursuing the matter on the facts that gave rise to the issue of the case being against public policy.

The ruling and determination of public policy was based on erroneous facts presented to the Court by the negligence of the previous solicitors.

That dismissal surely does not bar the Plaintiff from pursuing his claim based on the compromise reached on a debt owing a matter on which there has been no decision on the merits.

"Res judicata applied, except in special cases, to two situations: (a) in the strict sense, to points upon which the court was actually required by the parties to form an opinion and pronounce a judgment; and (b) in the

---

APPENDIX 26.3

4

wilder sense, to every point which properly belonged to the subject of litigation and which the parties, exercising reasonable diligence, *might have brought forward at that time."*

(See pg. 2 Lee Hiok Tng case cited in the 1st Defendant's Bundle of Authorities).

The claim herein on the compromise reached now is not against any public policy and it is not the point the earlier Court was called on to rule.

8. Looking at the 1st Defendant's first submission, it is clear that even the 1st Defendant was not pursuing his submission on the strict sense of res judicata.

The 1st Defendant in fact is seeking or rather taking a long shot of relying on the principal extended res judicata.

9. The extended principal of res judicata does not apply to the particular circumstances of this case. This is not a case where the issue ought to have been raised and has not been raised. Here is the situation where the issue was not determined at all because it never reached up to that stage.

APPENDIX 26.4

5

10.   The issue of extended res judicata is to be applied when there is abuse of process of Court. Here the compromise agreement has not been denied by the key persons namely Mr. Anthony Beeson and Kroll Investigation and they can therefore not in any way be regarded as an abuse of the process of Court.

11.   The Learned Registrar's finding that the compromise is an abuse of process to get around the time bar is rather speculative. In any way that is not a decision that can be made within the ambit of O. 14 r 12. As been pointed out, when the compromise agreement was made, there was no time bar to the original claim and there was therefore consideration for the 1st Defendant to enter into such agreement. The motive as to why the 1st Defendant wanted to enter into such agreement to compromise or what was the reasons for the 1st Defendant to enter into such compromise agreement are all matters of evidence to be determined at trial.

>   "*The principle of res judicata in its wider sense should be relied upon to avoid prolixity in litigation and to encourage early resolution of disputes. However it must be applied with the overriding consideration of working justice and not injustice. On the facts, the sellers should have been allowed to proceed with their second claim against the respondents.*"

(See case of Ng Chee Chong & Another v. Toh Kuow & Anor [1999] 4 SLR 45).

APPENDIX 26.5

6

12.   It would be grave injustice if the Plaintiff's case is not allowed to proceed with a proper hearing. If the Plaintiff is wrong, the 1st Defendant will be compensated by costs. No prejudice as such to the 1st Defendant.

13.   In any event in the earlier action (DC Suit No. 6013 of 1998) the matter was dismissed on a collateral issue of matter being against public policy. No decision was made on the fundamental determination as to whether the 1st Defendant owes the Plaintiff monies for work done.

> "In distinguishing a fundamental from a collateral one, the test is whether the determination upon which it is sought to found an estoppel is so fundamental to the substantive decision that the latter cannot stand without the former (see The Doctrine of Res Judicata (supra) at pp 181 – 182 para 211). Only if the answer is in the affirmative would the doctrine of issue estoppel apply."

(See pg. 18 of New Civilbuild Pte Ltd v Guobena Sdn Bhd & Another [2000] 2 SLR 378.

Dated this 11th day of July 2006

Solicitors for the Plaintiff
Messrs Vijay and Co.

APPENDIX 27

COPY

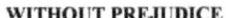

26/10/06.

26 Oct 2006

WITHOUT PREJUDICE

David Lim & Partners
50 Raffles Place, Singapore Land Tower #17-01
Singapore 048623

BY HAND

Attention: Mr Sunil Gil

Dear Sirs

OFFER FOR BOOK REVIEW

My company's claim against your client, *Signode (S) Pte Ltd* (who is related to the
Fortune 500 company, *Illinois Tool Works, Inc*) in DC Suit No. 3693 of 2005/W was
struck out on a point of law: quote from the judgement of the Learned District Judge:

> *"The cause of action in this case is founded on the compromise agreement – however, the
> consideration is for a forbearance to sue – which is to say, forbearance to sue on what?
> That links it all the way back to the 1998 Suit, which itself no longer exists, and to latch
> on to that as a cause of action would be res judicata in the extended sense and an abuse
> of process to get around the time bar. As a result, the compromise of 2002 lacks the basis
> of that consideration to begin with and therefore could not be a valid contract. I am
> therefore allowing the Defendant's application. The Plaintiff's claim is struck out".*

I would like to publish a book on this unhappy episode that caused severe emotional
distress to myself and made my company suffer a loss of over $400,000.00. I hope that
this book will draw the attention of the right people in the world who would be able to
persuade the CEO of *Illinois Tool Works, Inc (ITW)* not to use the legal approach to
ascertain whether my company should have been paid for services rendered in executing
an assignment successfully for your client - but rather a gentleman's approach as in
PRINCIPLE 7 of *ITW's* Statement of Principles of Conduct.

The book, titled DISMISSED WITHOUT TRIAL, focuses on all the events that led to the
filing of DC Suit No. 3693 OF 2005/W, communication between concerned parties, legal
documents filed in court and the legal arguments thereafter. To ensure that the contents
of my book are not erroneous, I am offering your client an opportunity to review it, with
an assurance to make the necessary amendments if I am unable to justify any of the
objectionable points raised.

Please let me know if you client is prepared to take up my offer within the next seven (7)
days from the date of this letter; failing which I would consider that your client has no
objections whatsoever to the publication of my book.

Yours faithfully

Gilbert A. Pereira
c/o 38A Jalan Pemimpin, #02-04 Wisdom Building, Singapore 577179

APPENDIX 28

DAVID LIM
& PARTNERS

advocates & solicitors • commissioners for oaths
notaries public • trademark & patent agents

your ref :
our ref : SU/2005-00581-5

STRICTLY PRIVATE & CONFIDENTIAL
TO BE OPENED BY ADDRESSEE ONLY

13 December 2006

Mr Gilbert Pereira
38A Jalan Pemimpin
#02-04 Wisdom Building
Singapore 577179

BY REGISTERED POST

consultant
TANG SEE CHIM

partners
DAVID T.L. LIM
YVONNE TAN
SURESH DAMODARA
AW EE TUAN
LEONARD HAZRA
KESAVAN NAIR
CHEONG CHUH FENG
JONATHAN FOONG
SUNIL S. GILL
JOANNA TENG
DIANA THE HUI LING

Dear Sir

DC SUIT 3693/2005/W

1. We refer to your letter to us dated 26 October 2006 and to your letter to our client dated 7 November 2006.

2. Notwithstanding the fact that 3 Subordinate Courts Judges and 1 High Court Judge have found that Absolute Tec has no valid claim against our client, you have threatened to proceed with the publication of material which could be defamatory of our client and also in contempt of court with a view to profiting from the same.

3. We further note your suggestion that our client or us as solicitors for our client "review" a particular document or letter which you intend to publish to the world at large and to point out any "errors" therein.

4. Your said suggestion is rejected. Our client refuses to associate itself with any such intended publication and reserves its right to take any steps necessary to protect its reputation, including but not limited to seeking recourse through the relevant authorities in Singapore.

5. For the avoidance of doubt, our client takes great objection to your threatened actions, including but not limited to the publication of potentially defamatory material, and nothing thus far is to be deemed as an acceptance by our client of your threatened actions.

6. We are also instructed by our client that you have contacted our client recently. Our client instructs us that any and all further communication between you and our client should be made through us as solicitors for our client.

7. Our client's rights are strictly reserved.

Yours faithfully

SUNIL S. GILL
DAVID LIM & PARTNERS

50 raffles place • 17-01 • singapore land tower • singapore 048623 • tel 65 **6532 2122** • fax 65 **6532 0122** • email **general@dlplaw.com.sg**
website **www.dlplaw.com.sg**

APPENDIX 29

review.

THE STRAITS TIMES THURSDAY, SEPTEMBER 11 2008

Lawyer bashing – with dose of humour

By K. C. VIJAYAN
LAW CORRESPONDENT

MR GILBERT Pereira just can't get over how much it costs to hire a lawyer.

Over eight years, he spent some $400,000 in a civil suit to recover $152,000 from a debtor – a personal disaster that nearly drove him to suicide. But the 49-year-old father of four told The Straits Times he staved off depression by turning to humour.

What's the difference between a good lawyer and a bad lawyer, he asks. "A bad lawyer drags out your case to make more money. But a good lawyer drags out your case even longer!"

Last month, he published a book of legal humour "judiciously titled", as lawyer Glenn Knight puts it in his preface, Factually Yes, Legally No. It was a reference to a recent debate on court acquittals: A person could be guilty of a crime but let off because the case against him can't be proved conclusively.

Mr Pereira quotes some famous names in his collection of legal jokes.

Like actor Cary Grant: "Divorce is a game played by lawyers."

Or American actor and writer Will Rogers: "Personally I don't think you can make a lawyer honest by an act of legislature. You've got to work on his conscience. And his lack of a conscience is what makes him a lawyer."

Or former United States president Theodore Roosevelt: "A man who never graduated from school might steal from a freight car. But a man who attends college and graduates as a lawyer might steal the whole railroad."

While lawyer disenchantment can be voiced in light form, MP Teo Ho Pin spoke of it seriously in Parliament recently. Six out of Singapore's top 10 fugitives listed in The Straits Times were lawyers who had disappeared with more than $28 million altogether, he noted.

(A re-check threw up seven lawyers among the top 10 fugitives, if Sivakolunthu Thirunavukarasu, who fled with about $2 million, is included.)

"This increasing trend of lawyers' misconduct and complaints is disturbing and of concern to the general public," Dr Teo said.

Four lawyer-MPs were quick to rebut his claims. Mr Hri Kumar Nair said: "It's because a vast majority of lawyers are honest and honourable that when one falls, it makes the news and the public expresses its surprise and outrage."

So are Singapore lawyers a bad lot or are we just talking about a few bad apples?

Former chief justice Yong Pung How once chastised the legal profession as a "naughty" one. That drew an apparent rejoinder from then-Law Society president Philip Jeyaretnam, who quipped: "We may not be the oldest profession in the world but, by gosh, we are a most naughty profession."

Three years ago, then-CJ Yong suggested the Law Society employ private investigators to track down lawyers who have absconded with other people's money.

The Law Society did not warm up to the idea, perhaps because of the costs involved. But taking the cue from the two businessmen who recently offered $1 million for information on terror fugitive Mas Selamat Kastari, lawyers may want to think of a bounty for lawyer-fugitives. It would be fitting to see errant lawyers nabbed and dealt with according to the law.

Otherwise, MPs can be expected to continue to complain about lawyers.

If nothing happens, there is still light relief from Mr Pereira for those seeking lawyer disenchantment therapy.

"What do you have if three lawyers are buried up to their necks in cement?"

Answer: "Not enough cement."

vijayan@sph.com.sg

APPENDIX 30

--- On **Fri, 16/1/09, gil pere** <*gil_pere@yahoo.com.sg*> wrote:

From: gil pere <gil_pere@yahoo.com.sg>
Subject: Facts of Case
To: "Wooten, James" <JWooten@ITW.com>
Cc: "Alison Donnelly" <adonnelly@ITW.com>
Date: Friday, 16 January, 2009, 10:52 PM

Hi James

Attached are the facts of the case involving Absolute Tec & Services Pte Ltd and Signode (S) Pte Ltd (formerly known as CS Packaging Corporation (S) Pte Ltd). The appendices have been left out as they are voluminous (over 100 pages of documents) but most importantly there are privileged and confidential information amongst them. As these appendices must be read in conjuction with the facts of the case to get the bigger picture, can I let Andre Accad - the managing director of ITW Singapore (Pte) Ltd to scrutinize them on your behalf. Alternatively, you may want to send me a return ticket to Illinois to bring the appendices and you may interview me at length to your satisfaction to establish the truth. I met Andre on 7 Jan 2009 and highlighted my plight. During the meeting, he assured me that ITW is a reputable company and always had honoured its dues to its vendors.

I sincerely hope that you would give your immediate attention in this matter as many people have suffered and continue to do so. My company never had its proper day in court because of lawyers who made good money instead of doing the right thing by advising Signode to settle our rightful dues.

Regards
Gilbert

Facts of Case.pdf (48.0 KB)

APPENDIX 31

From: tecnix [mailto:tecnix@singnet.com.sg]
Sent: Thursday, January 22, 2009 6:00 PM
To: Wooten, James
Cc: Donnelly, Alison
Subject: Complaint

Hi James

I replied to your email last Friday and have yet to receive any response from you that you had received it. Perhaps the email that I sent you from, which is a web-based email address, could not communicate with your email address. Hence, I am sending you the same using another email address.

Please do let me know if you have received my email and its attachment.

Regards
Gilbert

APPENDIX 32

Date: Thu, 22 Jan 2009 19:17:40 -0600

From: "Wooten, James" <JWooten@ITW.com>

To: tecnix@singnet.com.sg

Cc: "Donnelly, Alison" <adonnelly@ITW.com>

Subject: RE: Complaint

Attachments: *no attachments*

Mr. Pereira, I received your e-mail, although the appendices were not attached. I am reviewing your facts and will respond shortly. Thanks, James.

APPENDIX 33

-----Original Message-----
From: tecnix [mailto:tecnix@singnet.com.sg]
Sent: Friday, February 27, 2009 6:59 PM
To: Wooten, James
Cc: Donnelly, Alison; aaccad@texwipe.com
Subject: Outstanding Professional Fees

Dear James

It has been almost 5 weeks since we have communicated on the subject matter. With every day passing by, I am suffering consequentially as a result of my financial woes. My credit card bills are causing me to go into depression. My family has been affected and sometimes I am unable even to give them a decent meal.

I am not making any unreasonable demands but only am seeking your kind help to settle our rightful dues. I am sure you will do the right thing. I am still wondering why you are not requesting someone here in Singapore to exaimine the Evidence File which I have not included in the email that I sent you. You need to peruse this Evidence File if you want to be 100% convinced of my version of what happened here in Singapore. Please do understand that I cannot sent this Evidence File, which also include video recordings, because some of the documents are privileged and confidential. However, I am prepared to let a highly respected official from the US Embassy in Singapore to examine them. Alternatively, I can let Andre Accad to examine them on your behalf. Please advise.

Kindly acknowledge receipt of this email.

Regards
Gilbert

APPENDIX 34

```
----- Forwarded message from "Wooten, James" <JWooten@ITW.com> -----
Date: Mon, 2 Mar 2009 11:27:29 -0600
From: "Wooten, James" <JWooten@ITW.com>
Reply-To: "Wooten, James" <JWooten@ITW.com>
Subject: RE: Outstanding Professional Fees
To: tecnix@singnet.com.sg

Dear Mr. Pereira, I apologize for the delay in responding.  After reviewing the materials you
submitted, we have concluded that you are seeking payment of $152,000.00 for which there is
almost no support.  While you reference numerous attachments in support of your claim, it is
apparent you do not have documentation supporting the alleged increase in the contingency fee
to $200,000.00 or that the increased contingency fee would be paid without a successful civil
action against Peter.  Moreover, despite having filed three (3) legal actions against Signode,
no court has found merit in your claims.

Unfortunately, we have no personal knowledge of any of the facts surrounding your claim and,
therefore, can only judge your claim based upon the facts you have provided.  We regret to
inform you that the facts you have presented do not provide sufficient basis to pay your
claim.  We also received your request for a loan, however it is not a request that we can
honor.  Thanks, James.

James H. Wooten, Jr.
Senior Vice President, General Counsel & Secretary
Illinois Tool Works Inc.
3600 W. Lake Avenue
Glenview, IL 60026
Tel - 847-657-4206
Fax - 847-657-5206
```

APPENDIX 35

23 Jun 2009

BY REGISTERED POST

To the Kind Attention Of:

a. Mr Toh Boon Leng, *General Manager – Signode (S) Pte Ltd*
b. Mr Andre Acaad, *Managing Director – ITW (S) Pte Ltd*
c. Mr Tang See Chim, *Partner – David Lim & Partners*
d. Mr David Lim Teck Leong, *Partner – David Lim & Partners*
e. Ms Yvonne Tan Sok Chen, *Partner – David Lim & Partners*
f. Mr Suresh Damodara, *Partner – David Lim & Partners*
g. Ms Aw Ee Tuan, *Partner – David Lim & Partners*
h. Mr Leonard Hazra, *Partner – David Lim & Partners*

Dear Sir/Madam

Kindly vet the contents of this document. Objections raised on any part of this document that cannot be substantiated will be either withdrawn or amended accordingly. I sincerely hope that you will take this opportunity to set the record. If I do not hear from you within the next 7 days of this letter, I will take it to understand that you have no objections whatsoever to the contents contained herein.

Yours faithfully

Gilbert Pereira

INTERNATIONAL PRESS RELEASE

Contact: Gilbert A. Pereira
Tel: (65) 9383 2472
Email: gil_pere@yahoo.com.sg

CORPORATE DECEPTION: Fortune 200 Company distorts facts and conceals evidence. Lawyers submit false submission to court and resort to legal loopholes for client to evade payment for services received from private investigation agency.

APPENDIX 35.1

1.   I am a private investigator. My company, *Absolute Tec & Services Pte Ltd*, was appointed by *Signode [S] Pte Ltd* (a business unit of Fortune 200 Company, *Illinois Tool Works Inc*) in February 1998 to investigate its managing director (*MD*), who had tendered his resignation letter and was waiting to be released from the company with a handsome gratuity. *Signode* suspected he had breached his fiduciary duties and hence did not want to award him the gratuity. However, *Signode* did not have any proof on this and our job was to procure the evidence. Our professional fees included a contingency fee that was payable if our evidence was used successfully against the *MD* for breaching of his fiduciary duties in an anticipated legal action.

2.   After procuring evidence of breaches of fiduciary duties on the *MD*, *Signode* informed us it was advised by its lawyers not to take legal action against its *MD* due to a peculiar clause in his employment agreement that assured him double the stipulated gratuity if he were dismissed. Hence, *Signode*, armed with the evidence we had procured, decided to settle the matter privately and assured us our contingency fee would be still be payable, even if no legal action was taken against the *MD* – as long as its *MD* agrees to forego his gratuity as part of the conditions of its private settlement. Subsequently, the *MD* agreed to meet the stringent conditions imposed by *Signode*, which included forgoing his gratuity and reimbursing *Signode's* legal costs on a solicitor-client basis in the region of $60,000. We were congratulated for having done a good job and told to wait for the payment of our contingency fees.

3.   A few days later, *Signode* dropped a bombshell by stating that its shareholders were of the opinion that we were not entitled to our contingency fee as no legal action was taken against its *MD*. In order to add insult to injury, *Signode* claimed its lawyers informed its shareholders that the evidence we had procured did not proof that its *MD* had breached his fiduciary duties. As such, *Signode's* shareholders were only willing to pay us an ex-gratia amount for whatever work we had done. We refused to accept this amount but relented after *Signode* assured us that it will make up the balance amount of the contingency fee (amounting to S$152,000.00) through another business arrangement without its shareholders knowledge. In this arrangement, we were to purchase steel strapping at a stipulated price and resell them to *Signode* at a profit margin to cover the outstanding contingency fee that was due to us. After negotiating with many suppliers of steel strapping, we realized that we would never be able to get steel strapping at *Signode's* stipulated price. We informed *Signode* that this business arrangement was not workable and requested for the prompt payment of our rightful dues, failing which we would have no alternative but to resort to legal action.

4.   *Signode* challenged us to take them to Court, and gave us a veiled threat it would expose our covert operations in an open court. We did not bother about the veiled threat and brought *Signode* to Court. Unfortunately, we did not get a full trial as our claim was dismissed on a point of law. Whilst we were preparing to take a fresh action for a full trial to get all our evidence examined and witnesses questioned, *Signode*, now under a new management, claimed it was unaware of our contingency fee. It then offered to appoint *Kroll* (world's leading consultancy: *www.kroll.com*) to look into the matter - with the understanding we would be paid our contingency fee if *Kroll* was satisfied. We

APPENDIX 35.2

accepted the offer and *Kroll* came to our office to collect our working files and evidence on the *MD's* case. After about 2 weeks of investigations, *Kroll* expressed its satisfaction on our contingency fee and advised us to wait for its payment from *Signode*.

5.   Subsequently, *Signode* dropped a second bombshell - it blatantly refused to accept *Kroll's* findings and we had to resort to legal action again. *Signode's* lawyers, *David Lim & Partners (DLP)* flagrantly submitted to the Court that we had concocted the agreement involving *Kroll*. My company's lawyers, *Vijay & Company* argued this was a serious allegation as it imputed fraud on my company's part and urged the Court to order a trial for evidence to be examined and witnesses questioned to determine whether the said agreement was indeed a concoction! *DLP* argued that even if the agreement was genuine, it was unenforceable on two points of law, namely time-bar and *res judicata*. The Court accepted *DLP's* arguments and dismissed our case without a trial. Our lawyers then advised us that we could appeal to the High Court. We then sought advice from our circle of friends. One of them referred our matter to a senior lawyer (who wanted to remain anonymous as one of the senior partners of *DLP* is a close friend) and this was his comment:

> *"It is rather odd that the MD agreed to pay Signode its legal cost on a solicitor-and-client basis in the region of S$60,000 without even having been served any writ or a legal notice of intended action. The evidence against him must have been so overwhelming that he dropped his towel even before any proceedings could commence. It is an established fact that only the "very guilty" will agree to pay legal costs on a solicitor-and-client basis. Signode and its lawyers may say what they want but the conduct of the MD spoke volume."*

6.   According to the said senior lawyer, a travesty of justice was apparent in my company's matter. However, he advised us that appealing to the High Court may prove futile as *Signode*, with their deep pockets and legal battalion, are side-stepping the factual issues and relying heavily on technicalities and points of law that were not in our favour. As we were financially drained, we decided to drop our pursuit for justice through the legal path. Hence, I published a book, *Factually Yes, Legally NO!* – hoping to recover our losses through copies of its sales. Besides jokes on lawful humour, the book contains the true story that led to its publication, ie: the shameless conduct of *Signode* and *DLP* in my company's matter. Retailed at S$10.00 in major bookshops, it is also available through my website, *www.lawfulhumour.com*.

7.   I am also going to petition to the CEO of the parent company of *Signode*, namely *ITW Inc*, a Fortune 200 Company. I will be asking the CEO to re-look in my company's matter on compassionate grounds. I will also be urging him to investigate *DLP's* audacious and baseless submission to the Court that we had concocted the agreement involving *Kroll*. My petition letter-signing event will take place on 31 Jul 2009 from 1600 hrs to 1900 hrs at the Speakers' Corner (Hong Lim Park).

This international press release was offered to be vetted for its accuracy to the following persons. Amendments were made to objections raised that could not be substantiated with evidence: Mr Toh Boon Leng, *General Manager – Signode (S) Pte Ltd*, Mr Andre Acaad, *Managing Director – ITW (S) Pte Ltd* and the following lawyers from *David Lim & Partners*: Mr Tang See Chim, Mr David Lim Teck Leong, Ms Yvonne Tan Sok Chen, Mr Suresh Damodara, Ms Aw Ee Tuan and Mr Leonard Hazra

APPENDIX 36

50 Tagore Lane
#02-01 Markono Distri Centre
Singapore 787494
Tel : (65) 6468 9433
Fax : (65) 6468 6772
ACRA : 200102138N

ITW **Singapore (Pte) Ltd.**

Cleanroom Products

30 June 2009

Absolute Tec & Services Pte Ltd   **BY COURIER**
38A Jalan Pemimpin
#02-04 Wisdom Building
Singapore 577179

Attention: Mr Gilbert A. Pereira

With reference to your registered letter dated 23 June 2009, you are stating that if you do not hear from us 7 days that we have no objections whatsoever to its contents.

We would like to state again that we have no clues about this whole matter and cannot accept or deny your statement.

Thank you for your understanding.

ITW Singapore (Pte) Ltd

APPENDIX 37

An Invitation by Gilbert A Pereira
to sign his petition letter at
THE SPEAKERS' CORNER @ 31 July 2009 / 4 pm to 7 pm

LAWYERS GIVE FALSE SUBMISSION TO COURT.
FORTUNE 200 COMPANY DISTORTS FACTS AND CONCEALS EVIDENCE.

I am a private investigator. My company did an assignment for *SIGNODE (S) PTE LTD* to procure evidence against its managing director for breaching his fiduciary duties. Our evidence established his gross breaches of fiduciary duties; which resulted in him making an offer to forgo his gratuity of about $500,000 and reimbursing *SIGNODE* its legal fees on a solicitor-and-client basis of about $60,000, in lieu of all claims/actions against him. *SIGNODE* accepted his offer and then resorted to deception to avoid payment of our fees. We brought *SIGNODE* to court but did not get a full trial in the Subordinate Court as our claim was dismissed prematurely on a point of law. We appealed to the High Court and lost as the High Court ruled by our original pleadings that we had submitted to the Subordinate Court – which was subsequently established as defective.

Whilst preparing to get a new trial (after rectifying the defective pleadings), *SIGNODE*, now under a new management, claimed it was unaware of our outstanding fees of S$152,000. *SIGNODE* told us not to proceed with a new trial and offered to appoint world-renowned agency, *KROLL* (*www.kroll.com*) to look into the matter, with the view to pay us if *KROLL* establishes the said outstanding fees was genuine. We accepted the offer and *KROLL* carried out its investigations. Two weeks later, *KROLL* expressed its satisfaction and advised us to await payment of our outstanding fees. Lawyers then muddled the issues and we ended up in court again. *SIGNODE's* lawyers, *DAVID LIM & PARTNERS*, gave false submission to the Court that we concocted the agreement involving *KROLL* for the earlier mentioned purpose. To add insult to injury, they claimed that even if the agreement was true, we were not entitled to our fees based on points of law, i.e. "*time-bar*" and "*res-judicata*". We lost the case on these grounds and were advised to appeal to the High Court. As we were financially drained, we decided to drop our pursuit for justice through the legal system. I published a book, *Factually Yes, Legally NO!* – to help recover our losses through copies of its sales. Retailed at S$10 in major bookshops, it is also available at *www.lawfulhumour.com* (please call me for free delivery - Singapore only).

Sometime in January 2009, I made contact with *Mr James Wooten*, General Counsel of the parent company of *SIGNODE*, namely *ITW Inc*. I was pleased that he showed great interest in our matter, even after our three failed legal actions against *SIGNODE*. Another officer from *ITW Inc* reassured me that the previous three failed legal actions will have no bearing if we can prove that the said outstanding fees was due to us because *ITW Inc* is a honorable Fortune 200 Company and will not hide behind legal loopholes to avoid payment to its vendors. *Mr Wooten* then requested me to furnish evidence on the said outstanding fee. Subsequently, I sent him and *Ms Alison Donnelly*, spokesperson for *ITW Inc*, video footages of a meeting between officers of *SIGNODE*, namely its CEO and Finance & Corporation Planning Manager and officers from my company. In one of the video footages, *Signode's* high-ranking officers acknowledged the debt owing to us whilst in another blamed their lawyers for not taking action against the managing director for breaching his fiduciary duties (apparently for personal/selfish reasons, without considering the interest of the company). After these video footages were sent, I received a tip-off that *DAVID LIM & PARTNERS* took control of the matter from *Mr Wooten* and gave strict instructions that I should not be entertained. I believe this tip-off to be genuine because *Mr Wooten* and *Ms Alison Donnelly* never contacted me nor challenged the compelling video footage evidences that they had received.

I am now going to petition to *Mr David Speer*, CEO of *ITW Inc* to look into my company's matter as there has been a travesty of justice. I will also be urging him to investigate *DAVID LIM & PARTNERS'* false submission to the court that we had concocted the agreement involving *KROLL*.

GILBERT A PEREIRA
(tel: 9383 2472 / email: gil_pere@yahoo.com.sg)

PLEASE HELP ME UNCOVER THE TRUTH*!*
(documents/audio/video evidence available for inspection with prior notice)

APPENDIX 38

This is a sample of the letter that was sent out to the following on 17 July 2009:

Mr Russell Mark Flaum / Director of Signode
Mr John Michael Derek O'Callaghan / Director of Signode (S) Pte Ltd
Ms Juliet Ang / Secretary of Signode (S) Pte Ltd
Mr Toh Boon Leng / Director of Signode (S) Pte Ltd
Messrs David Lim & Partners
Ms Aw Eee Tuan / Partner of Messrs David Lim & Partners & shareholder of s company related to Signode (S) Pte Ltd

---

PETITION LETTER SIGNING EVENT @ THE SPEAKERS' CORNER

I am writing to you in relation to my attempts to recover S$152,000, being investigation fees owed to my company for undertaking an assignment for Signode (S) Pte Ltd sometime in the year 1998.

Enclosed herewith is my invitation letter to the public for the abovementioned event, which will be held on 31 Jul 2009 from 1600 hrs to 1900 hrs. This invitation letter will also be extended to the press in Singapore, USA, Australia and CEOs of multi-national corporations.

As the contents of my invitation letter has raised serious issues, you are requested to peruse it and raise any objections to any part(s) therein that you consider baseless and/or untrue. For clarifications, you may request for supporting evidence. I will make the necessary amendments to any objection(s) raised that cannot be substantiated. You are being given till 1700 hrs on 27 Jul 2009 to raise your objections/clarifications to the said invitation letter.

The objective of the abovementioned event is to garner support to persuade *Mr David Speer* (CEO of *Signode's* parent company, *ITW Inc*) to honour the findings of *Signode's* appointed consultant (in March 2002) that the earlier mentioned outstanding fee of S$152,000 was in fact due to us. However, if this objective can be achieved through your prior intervention, I will abandon this arduous exercise of mobilizing the masses and the press to help me put right the wrong done to us. And this would definitely bring about a closure to this saga expeditiously.

Yours faithfully

Gilbert A. Pereira

Enc.

APPENDIX 39

--- On Fri, 31/7/09, Suresh Damodara <damo@dlplaw.com.sg> wrote:

From: Suresh Damodara <damo@dlplaw.com.sg>
Subject: Re: Petition Letter Signing Event @ The Speakers' Corner
To: gil_pere@yahoo.com.sg, tecnix@singet.com.sg
Cc: "David Lim" <david@dlplaw.com.sg>, "Leonard Hazra" <leonard@dlplaw.com.sg>
Date: Friday, 31 July, 2009, 2:10 PM

Dear Sir,

Please see attached cease and desist letter which you should attend to it immediately.

Your faithfully,
Suresh Damodara
David Lim & Partners

50 Raffles Place #17-01
Singapore Land Tower
Singapore 048623
Direct : (65) 6531 0278
General : (65) 6532 2122
Fax : (65) 6532 0122
Email : damo@dlplaw.com.sg
Web : www.dlplaw.com.sg
GST Registration No. M8-8000139-6
UEN 53131093X

Ltr to Gilbert....pdf (134 KB)

APPENDIX 39.1

DAVID LIM
& PARTNERS

advocates & solicitors • commissioners for oaths
notaries public • trademark agents

Your ref :
Our ref : DL/DM/05-00581-5/tim

31 July 2009

Mr Gilbert A Pereira
c/o 38A Jalan Pemimpin
#02-04 Wisdom Building
Singapore 577179

BY E-MAIL, COURIER &
CERTIFICATE OF POSTING
(emails: tecnix@singnet.com.sg &
gil_pere@yahoo.com.sg)

Dear Sir

PETITION LETTER SIGNING EVENT @ THE SPEAKERS' CORNER

We refer to your letter dated 17 July 2009 (which we enclose herewith for your reference).

We would like to place it on record that on the 13th December 2006, we had put you on notice in respect of your threatened actions which we had maintained (and still do) were defamatory of our client, Signode Singapore Pte Ltd ("the client").

We now note that you have accused us as our client's solicitors in having submitted "false submissions to a Court of law in Singapore". These are serious and defamatory statements. Your statements are denied and we would like to put it on record that you have perpetrated defamatory remarks for the single purpose of extorting our client and ourselves of the sum of $152,000.00.

We would like to give you one more opportunity to:-

(a)   apologise to our client and ourselves in writing in a format agreeable to our client and ourselves;

(b)   cease and desist from all threatened and future conduct of this nature against our client and ourselves, and to provide a written undertaking in this regard and in a format agreeable to our client and ourselves; and

(c)   provide an undertaking to pay our client and us damages.

Please revert within the next 24 hours in respect of your agreement to the above, failing which our client and ourselves will have recourse to all our remedies at law.

Yours faithfully

David Lim & Partners

Enc
cc   client

APPENDIX 39.2

Gilbert A Pereira
c/o 38A Jalan Pemimpin
#02-04 Wisdom Building
Singapore 577179

**CERTICATE OF POSTING
& REGISTERED POST**

17 Jul 2009

David Lim & Partners
50 Raffles Place
#17-01
Singapore 048623

Dear Sirs

PETITION LETTER SIGNING EVENT @ THE SPEAKERS' CORNER

I am writing to you in relation to my attempts to recover S$152,000, being investigation fees owed to my company for undertaking an assignment for Signode (S) Pte Ltd sometime in the year 1998.

Enclosed herewith is my invitation letter to the public for the abovementioned event, which will be held on 31 Jul 2009 from 1600 hrs to 1900 hrs. This invitation letter will also be extended to the press in Singapore, USA, Australia and CEOs of multi-national corporations.

As the contents of my invitation letter has raised serious issues, you are requested to peruse it and raise any objections to any part(s) therein that you consider baseless and/or untrue. For clarifications, you may request for supporting evidence. I will make the necessary amendments to any objection(s) raised that cannot be substantiated. You are being given till 1700 hrs on 27 Jul 2009 to raise your objections/clarifications to the said invitation letter.

The objective of the abovementioned event is to garner support to persuade *Mr David Speer* (CEO of *Signode's* parent company, *ITW Inc*) to honour the findings of *Signode's* appointed consultant (in March 2002) that the earlier mentioned outstanding fee of S$152,000 was in fact due to us. However, if this objective can be achieved through your prior intervention, I will abandon this arduous exercise of mobilizing the masses and the press to help me put right the wrong done to us. And this would definitely bring about a closure to this saga expeditiously.

Yours faithfully

Gilbert A. Pereira

Enc.

RECEIVED
2 0 JUL 2009

APPENDIX 40

--- On Sat, 1/8/09, gil pere <gil_pere@yahoo.ccm.sg> wrote:

From: gil pere <gil_pere@yahoo.com.sg>
Subject: Re: Petition Letter Signing Event @ The Speakers' Corner
To: "Suresh Damodara" <damo@dlplaw.com.sg>, tecnix@singet.ccm.sg
Cc: "David Lim" <david@dlplaw.com.sg>, "Leonard Hazra" <leonard@dlplaw.com.sg>
Date: Saturday, 1 August, 2009, 12:43 PM

STRICTLY WITHOUT PREJUDICE

Dear Suresh

The subject event was held on 31 Jul 2009 from 4pm to 7pm. I was busy doing the necessary preparations and could not attend to routine stuff, like accessing my emails on that day. I am now looking at your email (1 Aug2009) and seek your advise on the relevance of this email as the said event had already taken place. Nevertheless, I deny the accusations stated therein. Your threatened actions are intimidating and tantamount to extorting me, by putting me under fear of legal action, for an apology and damages, for something that I had not done and never intend to do. I reserve my rights on this.

I take this opportunity to bring to your attention that my continued fight to right the wrong done to us is based, inter alia, on information received from your client's camp. I wonder whether there are two factions within your client's camp that are sending out differing messages! I would like the opportunity to meet up with your goodself to look seriously into this aspect, on a without prejudice basis. I hope you will take up this offer, which I believe will be in the best interest of your client and also your legal firm.

Regards
Gilbert

APPENDIX 41

Gilbert A Pereira
c/o 38A Jalan Pemimpin
#02-04 Wisdom Building
Singapore 577179

BY HAND

COPY

3 Aug 2009

David Lim & Partners
50 Raffles Place
#17-01
Singapore 048623

Attention: Mr Suresh Damodara

Dear Sirs

PETITION LETTER SIGNING EVENT @ THE SPEAKERS' CORNER

Further to your email of 31 Jul 2009 and my email of 1 Aug 2009 (copy of which is enclosed for your reference), I would like to reiterate my position as follows:

   (a)   your allegation that I have perpetrated defamatory remarks for the single purpose of extorting your client and yourselves of the sum of $152,000.00 is denied;

   (b)   your threatened actions are intimidating and tantamount to extorting me, by putting me under fear of legal action, for an apology and damages for something that that I had not done, and never intend to do.

Meantime, I refer to my letter dated 23 Jun 2009 (a copy of which is enclosed for your reference), which highlighted the above event that was to take place on 31 Jul 2009 from 4 pm to 7 pm. You were given ample time to raise your objections but chose to do so via an email at about 2 pm on 31 Jul 2009. I understand that you also sent a courier at around 3 pm on the same day during my absence. The said letter was sent to eight (8) parties, one of which was your goodself. Please note only *ITW* responded, claiming no knowledge of the whole matter and at the same time, neither accepting nor denying the truth of its contents.

I take this opportunity to request for a meeting with your goodself to allow me to present my case and proof to you that my remarks are not defamatory, as they are based on factual evidence. I trust that you will take up my offer, which is in the best interest of all parties involved. Please revert to this offer by 5 pm, 6 Aug 2009, failing which I will take it that you are henceforth in agreement with me that my remarks are not defamatory.

Yours faithfully

Gilbert A. Pereira

Enc

cc   Ms Nur Dianah Suhaimi
     SPH

APPENDIX 42

PETITION LETTER
to
Mr David Speer, The CEO, Illinois Tool Works, Inc
3600 West Lake Ave, Glenview IL 60026, USA

20 Aug 2009

Dear Mr David Speer

I am a director of *Absolute Tec & Services Pte Ltd*, a private investigation agency in Singapore. We did an assignment for one of your business entity, namely *Signode (S) Pte Ltd*. We completed our assignment successfully but did not receive full payment for our services rendered. After getting exasperated over false hopes that we would receive the balance amount of our fees (S$152,000.00) in due course, we resorted to legal action – which was unfortunately unsuccessful, due to technicalities.

As the legal path to recover our losses is no longer available to us, I published a book titled *Factually Yes, Legally NO!* (www.lawfulhumour.com) – hoping that the proceeds from the book sales can give us relieve from our financial woes. However, a good number of books have to be sold before we can recover our losses – and this may take a long time. I am hereby appealing to you for poetic justice. Kindly re-look into the matter. You will be convinced that we had been unfairly denied our fees after completing the assignment successfully for *Signode*.

I am sure you will do the noble thing once you ascertain the facts of this matter; especially whether the agreement made in March 2002 between my company and *Signode* is genuine. This is the agreement where *Signode* appointed *Kroll* (a renowned agency of Marsh & McLennan Companies, Inc - listed in the NYSE) to advise them on the validity of our claim – with the understanding that if *Kroll* was satisfied, we would be paid our fees – **which Kroll subsequently did after its investigations; they told us to await payment of our outstanding fees and not to resort to any court action.** However, *Signode,* through its lawyers, *David Lim & Partners* denied the existence of this agreement involving *Kroll*, and accused us of having concocted it. You may want to investigate why *David Lim & Partners*, after doing its due diligence, brazenly submitted false submission to the court that we had concocted the agreement involving *Kroll*.

Attached are the details of the matter. As the evidence are voluminous (notwithstanding the fact that most of them are in the hands of *Signode & David Lim & Partners*), I am ready to present them to you, if necessary. Please do let me know by 11 Sep 2009 whether you need any further information/verification before deciding to right the grievous wrong done to us. However, I prefer to resort to an amicable settlement and am prepared to close this unfortunate episode expeditiously if you could help me recover our rightful dues; the amount of which is a negligible sum for your esteemed Fortune 200 organization.

Yours faithfully

Gilbert A. Pereira

APPENDIX 43

Date: Tue, 1 Sep 2009 12:36:02 -0500

From: "Wooten, James" <JWooten@ITW.com>

To: tecnix@singnet.com.sg

Cc: David Lim <david@dlplaw.com.sg>

Subject: RE: Verification of document

Attachments: *no attachments*

Mr. Pereira, I understand that you tried to reach me earlier today to learn the status of your claim. Please be advised that we consider this matter to be closed. We recognize that you may not agree, but we do not owe nor will we pay you or your company the money you are seeking. Regards, James.

APPENDIX 44

DUPLICATE COPY

12 Jan 2011

Messrs David Lim & Partners

Dear Sirs   BY HAND

BOOK PROJECT – CORPORATE DECEPTION

Preparations are underway to publish my book, *Corporate Deception* (see enclosed draft flyer), based on a true account of what my company went through; salient points of which were made known to you and your clients, namely Signode (S) Pte Ltd and ITW Inc through meetings and/or telephone conversations and/or correspondences (letters/emails) in the past.

To avoid defamatory contents in my book, you and your clients are being offered the right to inspect the manuscript of my book before publication. I hope this offer will be taken up as there are information in my book that your clients did not had the opportunity to peruse, for e.g. my telephone conversation with your clients' senior executives, e.g. Pat Ficcione, etc. – as the discovery stage of my company's last action (DC 3693 of 2005) against your clients was thwarted through a summary dismissal (SUM 272 of 2006). These un-perused information will reinforce the fact that your clients were willing to consider my company's claim (for $152,000.00) even after it was summarily dismissed by the courts more than once; as your clients' new management were concerned that their previous management, comprising certain senior officials (whose services were abruptly disrupted – one of them committed suicide whilst under investigation for embezzlement whilst the other was terminated) could have submitted false evidence to short-change my company in the earlier mentioned summarily dismissed court actions. Hence, your clients engaged a world-renowned consultant (www.kroll.com) to investigate my company's claim – which culminated in their consultant confirming that my company's claim was bona fide and the amount of $152,000.00 being rightfully due to us.

My purpose of going into minute details in *Corporate Deception* is not to embarrass anyone, other than making my book marketable and saleable with intriguing facts – as I need to raise money to save me from the perils of my dire straits; caused by you and your clients. I am also appealing in my book to my readers to persuade your clients to have a change of heart and honor their own consultant's findings. I am sure your clients can afford to settle the rightful outstanding amount due to us, with costs, interest, etc – especially being an esteemed Fortune 500 company whose independent consultant had confirmed that my company is entitled to our claim of $152,000.00 for services rendered to your clients. If we can resolve this prior to the publication of my book, I would be grateful, as it would save me a great deal of mental and financial stress.

Meantime, if there is no possibility of an amicable resolution, please do let me know if you and/or your clients are keen to take up my earlier offer to inspect the manuscript of my book within eight days of this letter. Any objections raised will be taken into consideration for amendments to be made accordingly; failing which it would be deemed that there is no objections whatsoever by the parties whom this offer had been made available to.

Yours faithfully

Gilbert A Pereira
c/o 38A Jalan Pemimpin
#02-04 Wisdom Building
Singapore 577179

Enc.

c.c. Signode (S) Pte Ltd

       ITW Inc *through* ITW (S) Pte Ltd

"I'm still working on those briefs"

Lawyers
by
Margaret C Rigsby

I wonder how you sleep at night,
representing whether wrong or right
you tell me it is everyone's
right for counsel, defense.
Your ethics require you to
represent your client
to the best of your ability.

"I throw my client at the mercy of the court!"

ABOUT THE AUTHOR

Gilbert A Pereira, a former Police Officer, is a director of *Absolute Tec & Services Pte Ltd*, a private investigation agency. He has carried out various assignments for the man in the street to VIPs, small companies to multi-national corporations and government agencies; its high-profile case being the 1997 SilkAir crash in Palembang. Even after handling complex commercial and criminal cases successfully, *Gilbert* regards himself as a learner. According to him, the criminal mind is dynamic, and the investigator should never be complacent and allow the experiences to stagnate him.

Gilbert is also the author of FACTUALLY YES, LEGALLY NO! - a joke book on lawyers and their antics in Court. He is married to a childcare professional (who attained eternal life on 1 Jan 2013) and blessed with four children. *Gilbert* had always wanted to become a lawyer during his youthful days but had to abandon his ambition after his first-year law due to financial constraints. Despite his close encounters with unscrupulous lawyers and jokes about them in his earlier book, he still has the highest regard for this noble profession, though not necessarily the typical professional.